A Treasury of

Nostalgic Collectibles

Facts, Values, Background, Sources
and Societies of Popular Americana

by Charles J. Jordan

Published MCMLXXX by

YANKEE Inc.

Dublin, New Hampshire

This book has been prepared by the staff of
YANKEE, INC.

Clarissa M. Silitch, Editor

Margo Letourneau, Designer

FIRST EDITION

Second Printing

Copyright© 1980, by Yankee, Inc.

Printed in the United States of America
Library of Congress Catalogue Card No. 79-56573
ISBN 0-911658-04-1

Special Thanks

There are a lot of people I would like to thank in helping me put this book together. First and foremost, I would like to thank Clarissa Silitch, Editor of Yankee Books, who remained remarkably patient during the time I raced to meet deadlines and who remained calm when I handed her the typed copy of the Introduction five days before the book went to press. I'd also like to thank Margo Letourneau, Yankee's Art Director, who did a marvelous job of designing the book. Thanks also to Judson Hale, the Editor of Yankee *Magazine, who has been an encouragement to me by showing a continued interest in my material over the past nine years. I doubt that this book would have been realized if it wasn't for the great help I received from the many members of the staff at Yankee.*

I'd also like to say a special thanks to Esther Fitts, who first suggested I write a book, to the staff of the newspaper I was working for, the Coos County Democrat, *who put up with me during the production of the book, and to the collectors, who graciously introduced me to their fascinating world.*

This book is dedicated to my two sisters, Cynthia and Scotia, and our mother, who was the original collector.

Table of Contents

Section 4

Section 5

Section 6

Foreword

Writing about the collecting of memorabilia is as demanding a task as deciding on how to spell the noun commonly used to define that which is accumulated — namely, collectible, or collectable.* Our dictionaries shy away from a specific definition, merely listing the words as nouns at the end of a description of the verb, collect. Fortunately, the author of this interesting book has not dwelled on the semantics of spelling; rather he has zeroed in on the specifics which surround the assembling of items which reflect the nostalgia of our past.

We have always felt that to be involved in collecting of any type, one must know the rules just as a player of a game such as Monopoly must. Collecting is a game, a release for gambling instincts, a checkerboard requiring many moves (hoping all will be proper), and above all demanding stamina, fortitude, some intelligence and a willing pocketbook. This book supplies the information for the first-mentioned in a wide range of interesting items and at the same time infuses the reader with the confidence and desire to plunge deeper into the fascinating world of scholars and scoundrels. The author is not pedantic nor rigid in his examination of a various assortment of goodies; neither is he casual about the dangers of venturing into unsailed waters without being armed with facts, figures and above all, a sense of humility.

William Butler Yeats once said, "Think like a wise man but communicate in the language of the people." His admonition describes this book which will be well received equally by novice and old pro in the game of collecting.

George Michael
Merrimack, N.H.

*Ed. note: In our opinion the word "collectible" is a noun, the word "collectable" an adjective describing an object that is of collecting value. That is the usage followed in this book.

Introduction

Remember that Captain Midnight ring you had as a kid, and the copy of *Tom Swift in Captivity* you received one Christmas and read over and over again? Can you recall the time the King Brothers Show came to town, its arrival heralded by the appearance of all those colorful posters? What ever became of them? And what happened to that old box camera Father took your picture with on your first day of school, or for that matter, the old White Mountain Ice Cream Freezer Grandma would use to whip up homemade ice cream on hot summer days? And remember all those baseball cards you kept in a shoebox under your bed? Where have they all gone?

Well, the fact is that all these items have since entered the realm of collectibles. They are now considered "collector's items" and actively sought by collectors all across the country.

The 1970's saw a great rise in interest in antiques and collecting in general, a trend which continues into the 1980's. "More collectors than ever and a lessening supply of quality antiques resulted in more record prices being set than ever before in auction history," the *Boston Globe* said of the year 1979. The paper went on to say that a steady decline in the purchasing power of the dollar has led an increasing number of persons to put their money into objects rather than banks and bonds. "In short, the antique business is booming as it is about to enter the '80's."

Many people who may have never before considered collecting are taking their first serious look into antique journals. The immensity to which the collecting field has grown over recent years becomes clear when you scan the pages of a publication such as *The Antique Trader*. Practically everything appears to be collectable, from early dolls to tobacco tins. The prospective collector may find himself lost in a sea of objects and prices. It is the aim of this book to help sort out some of this confusion by acquainting the reader with some of the most popular collectibles currently being sought. I have deliberately steered away from the more traditional antiques, such as Chippendale furniture and bone china, as these have been considered collectable for most of this century and much has already been written about them. I have, instead, chosen items which have only recently gained full collectible status.

To familiarize the reader with these various collectibles, I have tried in each instance to provide some background information about the topic being covered in a particular chapter. I have included some of the prices certain items are currently going for, to give the reader an idea of what he should be expected to pay should he decide to enter the field.

If a person's budget is limited, he may want to try his hand at baseball card collecting, with many cards still readily accessible for as little as 25¢, or perhaps enter the field of sheet music, with many sheets dating back to the 1920's or earlier still to be had for under a dollar.

The more affluent person might choose to invest in silent-movie posters, which in many instances now exceed the thousand-dollar mark. Music boxes also require a sizable bank account. A Nicole Frères cylinder box, with six revolving cylinders, sells for $17,500. The reader must realize that all the prices given in this book are estimated to a 1980 market, and are subject to change with the passage of time.

In this book you will meet the collectors, people like banjo player Dan McCall of New York City, who has a collection of 50,000 individual song sheets stored in boxes in his living room from the floor to the ceiling, or collector Ed LeBlanc of Fall River, Massachusetts, who has three rooms of his home just filled with thousands of children's series books. These people will tell you that they all collect out of love, not money. They feel that if they make a little profit along the way, then that's fine.

The biggest question asked by people who become interested in collecting is "Where do I go to learn more?" — where to find others who also feel that early railroad objects, antique phones or early valentines are simply the most fascinating things ever created? To help in this area, I have provided the names and addresses of the existing associations formed for collectors of the subjects covered in this book. A letter to any of these groups will bring a response from someone who shares your interest and can tell you how to become a member.

So fill up your Orphan Annie Shake-Up Mug, take off your Buck Rogers Pocket Watch, put an early Paul Whiteman record on the Victrola, and sit back and relax as you get ready to enter the fascinating world of collecting . . .

Charles J. Jordan
Colebrook, New Hampshire
January, 1980

Section *1*

Remembrances
of Things Past

Circusiana

"A Sunburst of Bewildering and Perpetual Pleasures"

WHAT is circusiana? Anything to do with the six letters C-I-R-C-U-S — posters, heralds, couriers, program booklets, route books, circus books, and more. And what makes a collector collect circusiana? Love of the circus, primarily, but — "once you start collecting circusiana, it is hard to keep it just a hobby and not make it a way of life," an avid buff confesses. "I have circus advertising from the ceiling to the floor!"

Circus fans collect everything from vintage circus photographs to full circus costumes worn by aerialists, clowns and lion trainers. However, the most popular type of circusiana is undoubtedly paper circus memorabilia. It is in this area that one finds the greatest range of prices. For example, a 1953 King Brothers courier today is worth only $2, while original 1872 Stone & Murray Circus lithographed posters ("The Grand Finale" printed by Strobridge & Company of New York) are valued at $200 each.

Circus posters dating from the 1870's to the 1930's, during which period nearly all were produced by the lithographic process, are among the most valuable (and expensive) forms of printed circusiana. They are considered treasures of advertising art as well. Once plastered to the sides of barns, train depots and town hall buildings all across America, most circus lithographs measured 28 inches by 42 inches, which was the standard "one-sheet" size. A large number of two-sheet (56 inches by 42 inches) lithographs

Hand-colored circus posters are highly prized by collectors. This one bears the legend "H. A. Thomas Lith. Studio, 865 Broadway, N.Y."

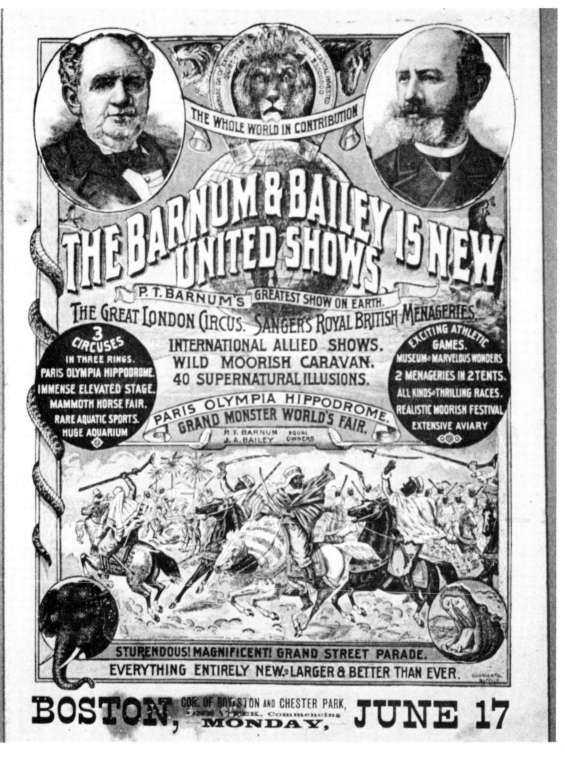

Elaborately colored and detailed couriers heralded the arrival of the circus well in advance of the date.

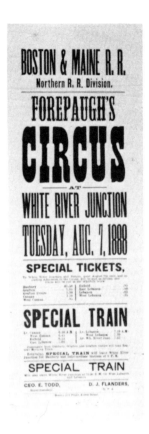

THE
Elephant,

ACCORDING to the account of the celebrated BUFFON, is the moſt reſpectable Animal in the world. In ſize he ſurpaſſes all other terreſtrial creatures ; and by his intelligence, he makes as near an approach to man, as matter can approach ſpirit. A ſufficient proof that there is not too much ſaid of the knowledge of this animal is, that the Proprietor having been abſent for ten weeks, the moment he arrived at the door of his apartment, and ſpoke to the keeper, the animal's knowledge was beyond any doubt confirmed by the cries he uttered forth, till his Friend came within reach of his trunk, with which he careſſed him, to the aſtoniſhment of all thoſe who ſaw him. This moſt curious and ſurpriſing animal is juſt arrived in this town, from Philadelphia, where he will ſtay but a few weeks.——————— He is only four years old, and weighs about 3000 weight, but will not have come to his full growth till he ſhall be between 30 and 40 years old. He meaſures from the end of his trunk to the tip of his tail 15 feet 8 inches, round the body 10 feet 6 inches, round his head 7 feet 2 inches, round his leg, above the knee, 3 feet 3 inches, round his ankle 2 feet 2 inches. He eats 130 weight a day, and drinks all kinds of ſpiritous liquors ; ſome days he has drank 30 bottles of porter, drawing the corks with his trunk. He is ſo tame that he travels looſe, and has never attempted to hurt any one. He appeared on the ſtage, at the New Theatre in Philadelphia, to the great ſatisfaction of a reſpectable audience.

A reſpectable and convenient place is fitted up at Mr. VALENTINE's, head of the Market, for the reception of thoſe ladies and gentlemen who may be pleaſed to view the greateſt natural curioſity ever preſented to the curious, and is to be ſeen from ſun-riſe, 'till ſun-down, every Day in the Week, Sundays excepted.

☞ The Elephant having deſtroyed many papers of conſequence, it is recommended to viſitors not to come near him with ſuch papers.

☞ Admittance, ONE QUARTER OF A DOLLAR.——Children, NINE PENCE.

Boſton, Auguſt 18th, 1797.

BOSTON : Printed by D. Bowen, at the COLUMBIAN MUSEUM Preſs, head of the Mall.

Above: *Railroad handbill announcing Forepaugh's 1888 circus.* Top right: *The very first American circus poster invited Bostonians in 1797 to view a "moſt curious and furpriſing animal."* Bottom right: *Circus poster lithographed in full color showing the daring exploits of star equestrienne, Miss Linda Jeal.*

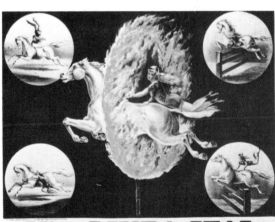

MISS LINDA JEAL,
"Queen of the Flaming Zone,"
ONE OF THE FEATURES OF P. T. BARNUM'S GREATEST SHOW ON EARTH.

P.T.BARNUM'S

New and Greatest Show on Earth coming by Four Special Trains.

were also produced. The Circus World Museum in Baraboo, Wisconsin, has even discovered a colossal hundred-sheet poster (19 feet by 50 feet), made to cover the entire side of a three-story building. Some of the best circus posters were produced by Strobridge & Company of New York (for Barnum & Bailey, Stone & Murray, and Sells Brothers), Courier Lithograph of Buffalo (for Ringling Brothers, Wallace Shows, and Buffalo Bill's Wild West Circus); the prolific Calvert Lithograph of Detroit and Gibson & Company of Cincinnati also deserve mention. Pre-1900 posters by these firms are considered the cream of paper circusiana.

The arrival of a circus was effectively proclaimed by vivid circus handbills, called "heralds." The average circus herald measured 28 inches by 10 inches. Unlike circus posters, heralds were seldom printed in more than two colors, making skillful use of detailed line engravings. They date back to the 1850's. Heralds provided their composers with a field day for hyperbole. One 1891 herald announced: "Ringling Brothers World-Wide, Radiating Realm of Recreation, a Sunburst of Bewildering and Perpetual Pleasures with America's Most Brilliant, Grand and Mighty Amusement fully a Century in Advance of its Contemporaries!"

Couriers, which first appeared in the mid-1870's, were broadsides similar in design to a newspaper. Inserted as supplements to

local newspapers within the vicinity of a show's scheduled appearance, they proved very successful — bringing news of the coming circus to rural homesteads along with the weekly paper. Some couriers contained fascinating articles, detailing (among other things) six easy exercises the circus strong man does every day "which you can do with a chair in your own parlor," and the favorite hymns of the Big Show's fat lady. Couriers dating from the 1870's and 1880's can bring $20 to $30 today. Printed as they were on newsprint, they are very hard to find in good condition.

Next to lithographed posters, circus route books are in the greatest demand among paper circusiana buffs. Route books provide a wealth of factual information about the early circus shows and are a gold mine to the circus historian and collector alike. Printed at the end of a season, they listed a day-by-day record of the stops made during a year. The 1946 Clyde Beatty route book is worth $6. The 1936 Tom Mix Circus edition is valued at $12. The John Robinson Circus route book of 1923 is going for $20, while pre-1900 Ringling Brothers route books start at $35.

Every circus goer is familiar with the circus program. These booklets repose in countless attics, kept as souvenirs of a day at the Big Top, and detail minute-by-minute activities in each ring. James Irving, "The Greatest Head Balancer," might be billed as performing in ring one, while "Cyclone," the trick mule, was kicking up a storm in ring two, and a troupe of clowns were in action in ring three. Programs originally purchased for 5¢ and 10¢ in the 1930's and 1940's, are now considered valuable circusiana. The 1950 Clyde Beatty program is worth $5, and the Barnum & Bailey program for the 1910 season gets $20 a copy. A 1935 Cole Brothers program is now a $10 investment.

Circusiana also encompasses books written about the circus, starting with the original circus bestseller, *Life of Barnum*, autobiography of the great showman. There were seven editions of the Barnum book spanning 1855 to 1891. Barnum offered the volumes for sale at his shows to the tune of $1.50 a copy and sold a hundred thousand a year. It was a runaway best-seller by the standards of the period. Because of this wide distribution, few copies are worth much today, usually getting only $5 to $10 at second-hand book stalls. Copies always merit scrutiny, however, as Barnum would on occasion personally sign copies of his autobiography on request. Signed copies, of course, have a much higher value. Some collectors aim to obtain all the successive editions of *Life of Barnum;* such sets command respectable prices.

Below: An 1870 hand-colored poster from one of P. T. Barnum's first New England tours.

Also collected by circus buffs are certain out-of-print volumes published within the past sixty years — elaborate circus picture books, children's stories, personal circus recollections and detailed histories of the various travelling shows are all popular. *The Ways of the Circus* by George Conklin (1921) brings $10 to $13, depending on condition. Circus bibliophiles are offering from $8 to $11 for *The Circus From Rome to Ringling* by Earl Chapin May (1932). Durants' *The Pictorial History of American Circus,* published in 1957 and considered "a bible" among circus fans,

Left: *Advertising cards featuring Jumbo — the greatest products promoter in circus history.* Below: *Jumbo put-together puzzle with original box.*

rarely sells for under $15 these days. The beautifully illustrated children's book *3 Rings* by Paul Brown (1938) is worth about $7.

Among other circus paper being collected are publicity photographs. Circus connoisseur Ted Haussman of Wellesley, Massachusetts, has accumulated twenty-six hundred autographed 8- by 10-inch glossies of circus clowns, high-wire performers, lion trainers and other circus celebrities. This remarkable collection, filling fifty-five scrapbooks, was begun by his father, the late Carl Haussman, a noted circus photographer in his own right.

Some of the earliest circus publicity photos being collected are those which were published in the *carte-de-visite* style of the mid-to-late nineteenth century. Collectors often report finding *carte-de-visite* photos of Mr. and Mrs. Tom Thumb in old family albums purchased at antique shows and flea markets, pasted in right beside those of beloved family relatives!

Circus band pictures also have acquired a sizeable following (many musicians got their start in circus bands, including big-band trumpeter Harry James). Even the stationery used by the old circuses is collected. The letterheads and envelopes of the various shows are just as brash and colorful as the big posters slapped yearly on barn walls.

Circus costumes are collected but difficult to obtain. Those that have entered collectors' circles were often presented by the family of a circus performer to a friend, and in time made their way into collecting circulation. James Hoye of Newington, Connecticut, has one of the more distinctive circus costume collections in the east, including high-wire aerialist costumes, bandmaster suits, a bear trainer's outfit and some nondescript costumes once owned by Terrel Jacobs, who billed himself as "The Lion King."

One coat in the Hoye collection is of particular interest, having been worn by the famous lion and tiger trainer, Clyde Beatty, the night he first went into the cage back in 1920. Beatty was working as a cage boy with a show when his big break came. He was a great animal lover and watched the training and performance of the mixed lion-tiger act by Pete Taylor. One night Pete became sick and couldn't go in the cage. Clyde was appointed to serve as his substitute and hastily given a band member's suit, the only uniform which could be found to fit him on such short notice. And the rest is history, according to Hoye — "Beatty went on to become the greatest lion and tiger trainer of all time, and this is the coat he wore on that first night in the ring." Stories like this prompt circus collectors to describe some items as "simply priceless." Irreplaceable, certainly. Complete costumes from within the past fifty years, for the most part, run from $200 to $500. Of course, costumes once belonging to circus celebrities will bring higher prices.

Interest in circusiana is being generated by such long-standing groups as the Circus Fans Association of America and the Circus Historical Society. The Circus Fans Association was formed in 1926 by a group of circus enthusiasts in Washington, D.C., hoping for "the preservation of the circus as an institution." Members assist circus show people when they arrive to perform in towns and cities across the nation. The group includes twenty-four hundred members nationwide, with the membership divided up by "tops" (state organizations) and "tents" (local town and city chapters). Annual dues are $12.50 for regular members, $5.00 for family members and $12.50 for affiliate members (circus personnel). Each chapter bears the name of a well-known circus personality of the past. There is the Buffalo Bill Tent in Davenport, Iowa, the Tom Thumb Tent in Norwalk, Connecticut, and the Bluch Landolf Tent in Hartford, the Charles Ringling Tent in Philadelphia, and 130 others. The group publishes its own bi-monthly magazine, "The White Tops," which keeps members up-to-date on association activities, circus appearances and circusiana information.

For more information about the Circus Fans Association, write to the office of Secretary-Treasurer J. Allen Duffield, P.O. Box 69, Camp Hill, PA 17011.

On the other side of the spectrum is the Circus Historical Society (2515 Dorset Road, Columbus, OH 43221), which concerns itself with perpetuating the memories of the glory days of the American circus. "The Circus Historical Society was founded in 1939 as an organization of collectors of circus material, including posters and programs," noted Fred Pfening, editor of the society's official publication, *The Bandwagon*. The Circus Historical Society now has around fourteen hundred members in the United States, Canada and a number of countries overseas and accepts as members any and all who are interested in the history of the circus.

Circus artifacts have been actively collected in this country for about fifty years now and have earned the right to stand beside such other time-tested antiques as Chippendale furniture and pewter snuff boxes. Yet circusiana remains a continually growing field, with the collector's items of tomorrow found wherever there is a circus today. Trucks may have taken the place of the old-time circus trains, and shows may now appear in civic centers rather than tents — but the circus still provides uniquely exhilarating entertainment and excitement for "Children of All Ages." □ □

The Silent Screen

These memorabilia are among the rarest of all

Above: *Movie magazines from the Twenties and Thirties are eagerly sought. Covers here left to right feature Loretta Young, Katharine Hepburn, and Joan Crawford.*

Below: *Paramount magazine advertisement for original (1926) movie version of Beau Geste.*

P ERHAPS you caught Charlie Chaplin in *The Gold Rush* at the Majestic Theater in Butler, Pennsylvania, in 1925. Or were one of the many who thrilled to *The Mark of Zorro* (1920) with Douglas Fairbanks at the Pastime in Duncan, Oklahoma. You may have seen Lillian Gish in *Broken Blossoms* at the Rialto of South Norwalk, Connecticut, in 1919, or in its sixth week at the Dreamland in New Haven. Folks in Yakima, Washington, may recall Mary Pickford in *Rebecca of Sunnybrook Farm,* which played at the Empire Theater in 1917 just about the same time that the Strand in Peabody, Massachusetts, was featuring Theda Bara in *Cleopatra.* Crowds would line up outside neighborhood theaters hours before each showing of these and other now legendary motion pictures of the silent era. Today these names on movie memorabilia are valid passports to the world of classic silent "cinemabilia."

Most of the silent stars of fifty to seventy-five years ago are gone. But their popularity is as great today as it was then, when many a pianist wore out keyboard and fingers trying to keep up with Pearl White in *The Perils of Pauline.* If you doubt it, just ask one of the hundreds of members comprising the Society for Cinephiles, the largest of many groups of active silent film collectors. "Devoted to the History and Enjoyment of the Movies," Cinephiles (national headquarters at 2835 North Sixty-first Place, Scottsdale, AZ 85257) gather in a different corner of the country each Labor Day weekend to view early films around the clock, talk about their collections, and exchange cinemabilia with one another. And, inevitably, whenever silent film buffs gather, the topic of conversation leads to "those lithographed treasures" — silent movie posters.

Talking with a cinemabilia collector, you come away feeling that no other twentieth-century Americana is more sought after than silent-movie posters.* "Silent-era posters are very much in demand," one collector told me, "because they are becoming more and more scarce. The few that are offered from time to time go for astronomical prices." Color lithos of Douglas Fairbanks in *Robin Hood* are pulling in a swashbuckling $100; posters of *Ben Hur* featuring Francis X. Bushman are worth $250; posters showing Lon Chaney in *The Phantom of the Opera* have netted as much as $300 apiece. Most collectors agree that posters for Charlie Chaplin's earliest Keystone and Essanay films (1914-16) and Mary Pickford's first Biograph movies are the most valuable — in top condition being worth well over $1000.

In mounting movie posters for display (or any valuable printed-paper Americana for that matter), one should attempt to prevent acidification. Though acidification is more of a problem when dealing with old newspapers, it has been known to take its

Below, left: Top, lobby card; bottom — movie poster. Right: From upper left, 1926-27 souvenir film programs and pressbook from MGM, Pathé and Paramount, and May 1924 Film Fun *magazine.*

*Sound-film posters are also gradually sliding into the realm of collectibles — you can start almost anywhere. Poster catalogues advertised in *Classic Images* are billed as listing "thousands priced from $5 to $3000."

toll among the earliest paper cinemabilia, printed as they were on cheap grades of paper. Whenever ink and cheap paper are involved, acidification can result. This happens from extended air contact, which works in conjunction with the elements in the ink to discolor and decay the paper. The best way to preserve valuable paper items like movie posters is to sandwich the poster between two sheets of clear acetate before framing it under glass. This safeguards the paper from both air contact and damage due to careless handling. Acetate can be purchased from larger stationery stores or camera shops for about $4 a 30-inch by 24-inch sheet — a small price to pay to protect a $200 or $300 investment.

With original posters so high-priced, many collectors concentrate on the more accessible items of silent-screen cinemabilia. Lobby cards and "scene stills," the graphics displayed in glass cases inside theater lobbies, are still within reach of most collectors. Lobby cards (measuring 11 by 14 inches) were miniature posters, with tinted-color pictures. Usually issued in sets of eight, individual lobby cards can now be found for under $25, as buffs seek to complete sets. Scene stills (not to be confused with

Above: *Paramount magazine advertisement.*

publicity photos) are very popular with collectors. Some enthusiasts have built up still collections of more than a thousand scenes from various films.

Many collectors specialize in printed forms of silent cinemabilia, such as pressbooks, photoplay book editions, and early movie magazines. Originally issued to movie theater owners, pressbooks are sought today because they contain a wealth of promotional art and provide an "inside" look into the craft of film publicity. Pressbooks contained "mats" for newspaper advertising and clever suggestions for boosting patronage. One suggestion was that local theaters sponsor Rudolph Valentino and Theda Bara look-alike contests, thereby attracting sheiks and vamps from miles around.

Photoplay book editions, which appeared around 1917 and flourished until the end of the silent era, were novelized versions of popular motion pictures illustrated with black and white stills from the films and full-color dust jackets. At the height of the photoplay editions' popularity, Grosset & Dunlap led the field in the number of books published. Among the volumes on Grosset & Dunlap's list in the early twenties were *Riders of the Purple Sage* by Zane Grey, *The Covered Wagon* by Emerson Hough, *The Dramatic Life of Abraham Lincoln* by A.M.R. Wright, and Booth Tarkington's *Penrod*. "All illustrated with scenes from the photoplays" promised the publisher. As more and more cinemabilia collectors strive to compile libraries of stories both popular and obscure which saw celluloid transformations, demand for these books is increasing. A copy of John Monk Saunders' *Wings* (1927) starring Clara Bow and Charles Rogers, is worth $8, while MacMahon and MacPherson's *The Ten Commandments* (1923) with twelve Paramount stills brings $12.

Then, as now, books were often fleshed out from the screenplay after a film had been produced, to capitalize on the movie's box-office popularity. *The Freshman,* based on Harold Lloyd's motion picture of the same name released by Pathé, was novelized by Russell Holman in 1925. "Millions have enjoyed the clean, wholesome fun of Harold Lloyd upon the screen," the book's jacket read. "At last the rollicking humor of the famous star has been caught in a novel, written directly from his greatest picture, *The Freshman*." In Holman's novelized version, we find the hapless Harold on a train sitting next to a young woman trying to complete a crossword puzzle:

> *I know the word for 19 vertical — "a name for one you love"* [Harold says]. *It's "sweetheart." She shook her head. "Darling!" he suggested. That didn't fit either. "Dearest!" he cried triumphantly. "Precious!" she countered. "Honeybunch!" "Sweetie!" Then he felt a hand fall upon his shoulder and turned around. A sweet, motherly-looking elderly lady had laid a hand upon him and another upon the amazed girl beside him and was saying in a blissful voice, "Isn't it wonderful to be in love?"* *

* *The Freshman,* by Russell Holman, Grosset & Dunlap, N.Y. 1925, p. 89.

THE
"ROUGH RIDERS"

A
VICTOR FLEMING
PRODUCTION
with
MARY ASTOR, CHARLES FARRELL
GEORGE BANCROFT AND
ALL STAR CAST
Story by HERMAN HAGEDORN

The most picturesque band of adventurers in American History recruited from every walk of life in the stirring days of '98 lives again in a picture as great in scope and power as "The Covered Wagon." Coming soon.

Above: *Paramount magazine advertisement.*

Life was so much simpler back then.

Then there were the movie magazines of the period, with articles telling all about the people of the silent kingdom. Publications like *Motion Picture, Movie Weekly, Motion Picture World, Picture-Play, Photoplay,* and *Motion Picture Classic* are a few of the old glossy magazines being collected today. Their covers display the young and sentimental faces of the Hollywood of over fifty years ago. Mary Pickford beams on us from the August 1919 cover of *Motion Picture;* Norma Talmadge adorns the June 1926 *Picture-Play;* John Barrymore dominates the cover of the November 1926 issue of *Motion Picture Classic.* Sooner or later everybody who was anybody in Hollywood appeared on a glossy cover. The stories in these magazines were pure Hollywood jewels.

Photoplay was the most sensational, taking its readers to visit actress Fannie Ward's spectacular new home ("the most sumptuous photoplayer's domicile in the world") or poolside with "The

Sooner or later everyone who was anyone in Hollywood showed up on the cover of one of the movie magazines.

Above: *Paramount magazine advertisement.*

Swimming Pools of Hollywood." Stories about Rudolph Valentino guaranteed sure-fire newsstand sales — during his life and after. The great Valentino penned a story for *Photoplay* in the twenties called "Woman and Love," in which he surmised that "a love affair with a stupid woman is like a cold cup of coffee." After Valentino's untimely death in 1926 the stories about the great lover increased. ("Does Rudy Speak from Beyond?" asked *Photoplay.* "Natacha Rambova tells of the spirit messages she claims to have received from Valentino.") Another article informed readers that the middle name of the rough-and-tumble silent screen cowboy William S. Hart was "Shakespeare." No wonder he went through life with two six-shooters in his hands! Copies of *Photoplay* from the 1920's sell for $4 to $8 if in good condition.

There are many publications — letters, newspapers, and magazines — which cater to the interest of collectors of motion-picture artifacts. The leader has been *Classic Film Collector,* which for years was published in Pennsylvania, providing early screen buffs with an abundance of articles about the silent years — such as "Collecting Chaplin," "1918 Flickers and Movie Folk," "Hollywood Doings of 1925," to name a few found in recent issues. In 1978 *Classic Film Collector* was purchased by Blackhawk

The value of old movie magazines to collectors depends on
the cover personality as well
as on the date and the actual
condition of the magazine.
Far left — Rudolph Valen-
tino and cowboy hero
William S. Hart.

SOME EXAMPLES OF STARS FEATURED ON COVERS OF EARLY MOVIE MAGAZINES

MOTION PICTURE

DATE	STAR ON COVER
June 1918	Corinne Griffith
July 1918	Alla Nazimova
Nov. 1918	William S. Hart
April 1919	Anita Stewart
July 1919	Dorothy Phillips
Aug. 1919	Mary Pickford
Jan. 1920	Mae Murray
Mar. 1920	Aneth Getwell
July 1920	Blanche McGarity
Oct. 1920	Mildred Harris Chaplin
Dec. 1920	Hope Hampton
Jan. 1921	Mary Pickford
Feb. 1921	Norma Talmadge
Mar. 1921	Ruth Roland
Apr. 1921	Pearl White
Sept. 1921	Douglas Fairbanks
Dec. 1922	Mae Murray
Feb. 1923	Lila Lee
Mar. 1923	Pola Negri
June 1923	Anna Q. Nilsson
Nov. 1923	Eleanor Boardman
Mar. 1924	Colleen Moore
May 1924	Baby Peggy
July 1924	Pola Negri
Aug. 1924	Betty Compson
Sept. 1924	Anna Q. Nilsson
Nov. 1924	Mae Murray

PICTURE-PLAY

DATE	STAR ON COVER
Feb. 1922	May Macavoy
May 1922	Louise Wilson
June 1922	Patsy Ruth Miller
July 1922	Alice Terry
Oct. 1922	Madge Kennedy
Nov. 1922	Leatrice Joy

MOTION PICTURE CLASSIC

DATE	STAR ON COVER
July 1923	Richard Barthelmess
Sept. 1923	Norma Talmadge
Oct. 1923	Alice Terry
Dec. 1924	Mme.Nazimova
Jan. 1925	Jackie Coogan
Apr. 1925	Louise Fazenda
July 1925	Norma Talmadge
Jan. 1926	John Gilbert
June 1926	Clara Bow
Nov. 1926	John Barrymore
Jan. 1927	Alice Joyce
Mar. 1927	Betty Bronson
June 1927	Billie Dove

Films, Inc. (the foremost producer of silent movies for home screens in the world) and moved to Iowa. The publication's founder, Samuel K. Rubin, has remained on as editor, but the name has been changed to *Classic Images*. "The plans are to increase circulation and make my former hobby into a profitable publication," Rubin said. *Classic Images* is currently published quarterly at $2 a copy, the address is P.O. Box 4079, Davenport, IA 52808.

An up-and-coming publication for film buffs is *Film Collector's World,* published since August 1976 at P.O. Box 248, Rapid City, IL 61278, twice monthly. This magazine has a readership of about seven thousand film collectors. Subscription rates are $10 a year (twenty-four issues). The publication features informative articles about early motion pictures and film production. In one recent issue, the reader was treated to a tour of the backlots of MGM, 20th Century-Fox, and Universal studios. The publication also collects and reprints pertinent articles from newspapers around the country.

Also popular with cinemabilia collectors are home-movie versions of the silent classics. Leaders in vintage film reproductions for home screens are Blackhawk Films (Dept. 5262, Davenport, IA 52808), and the Milestone Movies Corporation (P.O. Box 75, Monroe, CT 06468). Depending on the title desired, either highlights from the film or the complete film (or both) are available in 8 mm, in black and white and (sometimes) color. These have more value as entertainment than as collectibles, though black-and-white films kept in good condition will probably appreciate in value with time. (The life of a color film print is only about ten years — after that time it will begin to fade.) Catalogues are available from both Blackhawk and Milestone.

On October 6, 1927, talking motion pictures arrived with Warner Brothers' *The Jazz Singer* starring Al Jolson. The first movie to feature a sound segment, it shook the movie world like an earthquake. Sound was the wave of the future and moviehouse owners rushed to equip their theaters for "talkies." Many silent screen stars found their careers ended with the coming of sound. No matter how striking a leading man might appear on film, if he spoke his lines in a high-pitched voice, he just didn't make it. And if the diminutive starlet sounded like a truck driver, she was soon packing for home as well.

The Jazz Singer closed the curtain forever on the silent screen, but not for collectors! □ □

Those Sunday Funnies

Enjoy, but handle with care

T HE Sunday funnies — those light-hearted color creations in which countless Americans seek refuge in the face of another Monday — have been with us a long time, more than eighty years in fact. And week after week, for an estimated forty-three hundred consecutive Sundays, we have shared in the joys and sorrows of our favorite characters. From "The Katzenjammer Kids" to "Peanuts," the American comic strip has become a way of life.

Enthusiasm for the old color comic has given rise to a special breed of collector — the comic-art buff. There are two types of Sunday funnies fans — those who collect the high-priced original artwork panels from which the strips were duplicated, and those with lower budgets who collect the printed copies of the strips from the newspaper comic sections.

Original drawings, of course, command the most spectacular prices. One collector recently unearthed ninety-five "Bringing Up Father" drawings of the 1910-1920 period, which he sold for $20 to $25 apiece, only to discover later that they were worth up to $100 each! Original drawings by Frank King for early "Gasoline Alley" strips are worth between $300 and $1000. Herriman's "Krazy Kat" originals bring anywhere from $600 to $800 and Segar's "Thimble Theatre" and "Popeye" drawings are valued from $500 to $2000 or more. The original artwork for a 1909 "Little Nemo" Sunday strip was recently advertised at $2500.

Price ranges like these are out of reach for average collectors, most of whom concentrate on the printed newspaper pages, known as "tear sheets."* These pages require careful handling, as they are often very brittle and yellowed with age. Tears and stains detract from the value; an over-zealous sweep of the hand can turn a rare sheet of "Little Nemo in Slumberland" worth $50 in good condition into a torn piece of paper worth less than 50¢. One of the best publications for collectors in this field is *The Buyer's Guide for Comic Fandom* (15800 Route 84 North, East Moline, IL 61244). Editor Alan Light says his publication (which he terms an "adzine") reaches over ten thousand readers each week. An average issue runs 72-140 pages; a subscription costs $16 a year. Individual sample copies may be ordered at 50¢ each. Every issue of the "adzine" is chock full of ads placed by comic art collectors from all corners of the country, news of interest to collectors, book reviews, and announcements of up-coming shows and conventions for comic art buffs.

Tear sheets from the years between 1896 and 1929 are of the greatest interest to collectors, as this was the period of the fastest

---

*The term "tear sheets" refers to whole pages of a newspaper, *not* portions torn out from such pages.

Remembrances of Things Past/*Sunday Funnies*

Good clean tear sheets of Happy Hooligan's adventures in the Twenties bring $4-$8.

growth for the American comic strip. Outcault's "Yellow Kid" made his illustrious debut in 1896, in the only newspaper then beginning to experiment with color printing. By the time we were singing "Barney Google, with his goo-goo-googley eyes" in 1924, more than three hundred papers across America ran full-color comic supplements weekly. Among the classics of that period sought by collectors today are the following:

The Yellow Kid. Early in the 1890's the *New York World* began trying out a newly devised process of color printing. The first attempts by the *World* were hindered by the unfortunate tendency of the yellow ink to run. When the problem was finally solved in 1896, the newspaper celebrated by printing a comic drawing by staff illustrator Richard Outcault (1863-1928) entitled "Golf — the Great Society Sport as Played in Hogan's Alley." Appearing in flawless color on January 5, 1896, it centered around a group of city street kids playing golf. And there, right in the middle, was a little boy in a bright yellow nightshirt. It all would have ended right there but for one thing — the readers' response was ecstatic! The *World's* editors then set Outcault and other illustrators to work on a batch of comical drawings for a new color supplement. The *World Sunday Comic Weekly* appeared, and a new art medium was born.

Cover of the Aug. 7, 1898 World Sunday Comic Weekly. The artists worked in pen-and-ink, with three overlays to show the printer the distribution of each color. Color could be either screened or solidly printed (rarely done today). The solid reds and yellows on this sheet still glow as brightly today as when they were printed.

Many pioneering creations filled those historic issues: Richard Outcault's "Yellow Kid," "The Little Nippers" by George B. Luks, Frank H. Ladendorf's "Mischievous Willie," and the W. W. Denslow creation, "Father Goose." Also noteworthy were silhouettist J. K. Bryans' strip, "The Kidlets," "The Roly Polys" by Paul West, and J. B. L.'s "The Barnyard Club." *World Sunday Comic Weekly* sheets dating between 1896 and 1900 are avidly sought by collectors everywhere. Considered very rare, complete, well-preserved copies have sold at prices ranging from $75 to $300.

The Katzenjammer Kids. The longest continuously published comic strip, "The Katzenjammer Kids" got under way on December 12, 1897, in the *New York Journal*. Drawn by Rudolph Dirks (1877-1968), the series standardized two cartoon innovations — the sequence panel and the "word balloon." Dirks continued to draw Hans, Fritz, Mama, the Captain and the Inspector for the *Journal* until 1912, when a contract dispute led him to move over to the *World*. Having secured the rights to the name "The Katzenjammer Kids," the *Journal* hired another cartoonist, H. H. Knerr, to continue it. Meanwhile, Dirks kept on drawing his characters in a strip published in the *World* as "The Captain and The Kids." Today both strips are still being published (drawn by

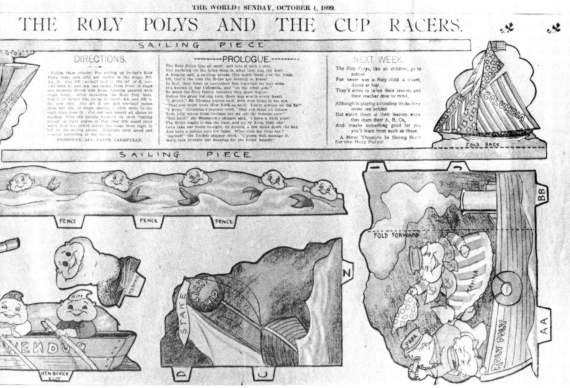

"The Roly Polys" by New York World *cartoonist Paul West, Oct. 1, 1899. These cut-outs are part of an on-going series; each week new pieces were offered for the reader to cut out and add to a cardboard stage and other pieces already assembled.*

other cartoonists) by King Features Syndicate and United Features Syndicate, respectively. Most desirable to collectors are the pre-1912 Katzenjammers drawn by Dirks for the *Journal*. Of course, as is the case with nearly all comic strips, the initial, or "debut" episode (1897) is the ultimate collectible.

Happy Hooligan. Created by Frederick Burr Opper in 1900 for the Hearst newspapers, Happy Hooligan entertained Americans with his misadventures for many years in such papers as the *New York Journal, San Francisco Examiner,* and *Boston Sunday Advertiser.* Happy was a not-too-bright chap who wore a tin can for a hat. Good, clean tear sheets of "Happy Hooligan" range in price from $4 to $8 for common 1920's episodes, and up to $25 for the earlier, scarcer sheets — indeed up to $100 could be asked for one of these in mint condition, which is very difficult to find today.

Buster Brown. Richard Outcault left the *World* in 1898 when his "Yellow Kid" cartoons were discontinued and eventually ended up at the *New York Herald.* Here, on May 4, 1902, he launched his most famous comic character, "Buster Brown." On the surface, Buster seemed to be the complete opposite of Outcault's earlier creation, being a spotless lad all done up in a red Fauntleroy suit. But actually he was just the same sort of mischievous fellow as the Yellow Kid. Buster and his dog, Tige, romped through twenty-four years of Sunday funnies and brought their creator a small fortune in royalties from a St. Louis company which used the pair in advertising its line of "Buster Brown" shoes. "Yellow Kid" cartoon panels being so rare today, most collectors are eager to acquire "Buster Brown" tear sheets as the next best thing. And it doesn't stop there. A like-new pair of 1906 "Buster Brown Blue Ribbon" patent leather shoes in the original box recently sold at a comic art convention for $36!

Little Nemo in Slumberland. Artist Winsor McCay was one of the most creative talents ever to sit before a cartoonist's easel. His classic "Little Nemo in Slumberland" debuted in the *Herald* on October 15, 1905, and ran sporadically for twenty years. The comic strip centered around a little boy named Nemo who had some of the most remarkable dreams imaginable. Nemo's dreamworld was filled with bizarre scenery, leprechauns, dragons and creatures from out of this world. Nemo always woke up at the end — usually by falling out of bed and bumping his head! "Little Nemo" panels are truly works of art and are valued among the highest by collectors. "Little Nemo" tear sheets can bring $35 to $60 or more. The debut tear sheet has brought over $100.

Boob McNutt. Boob's name gives us a good idea of the type of character he was, the perpetually bumbling buffoon who "wasn't playing with a full deck." His creator, Rube Goldberg (1883-1970), was perhaps the most prolific of all the early cartoonists. "Boob McNutt" was first published by the McNaught Syndicate in 1916 and had a long and prosperous run. All Rube Goldberg's works are cherished bits of timeless humor, including the popular panels "Mike and Ike, They Look Alike," "Lala Palooza," "Professor Butt's Inventions" and that perennial favorite, "Foolish Questions." His "Foolish Questions" featured

The Dec. 9, 1900 Sunday World celebrated the expansion of its "Funny Side" to eight pages with cameo photos of its cartoonists accompanied by samples of their creations. R. Outcault is seen center; Paul West, far right.

witty comebacks to ridiculous questions. One showed a man at the doorstep of a house which had a large "99" above the door. Man: "Is this number 99?" Woman: "No, mister, it's number 66 — we turned the house upside down just for a change." Another classic showed a man driving a battered automobile. Pedestrian: "Have an accident?" Driver: "No, thanks, just had one."

Gasoline Alley. What started out as the story of a group of auto enthusiasts who met in a back alley to discuss automotive topics, turned into the great family epic, "Gasoline Alley." Creator Frank King introduced a surprising innovation to the funnies with this strip, whose debut occurred November 24, 1918 — the characters of "Gasoline Alley" actually grew up, had families and got old, just like the readers. On February 14, 1921, character Walt Wallet found an infant left on his doorstep, took him in, and named him Skeezix. The baby learned to walk and talk, endured adolescence, grew into manhood, became a GI in World War II, got married, had children and in time became a grandfather. Many collectors treasure "Gasoline Alley" panels as one would photos in a family album. Strips from the 1920's run from $5 to $8 each.

Thimble Theatre. In 1919 cartoonist Elzie Segar went to New York to propose a comic strip to the King Features Syndicate. He got a contract. The strip was "Thimble Theatre," and it told the story of the scatterbrained Oyl family. The main characters were Olive, Castor, Cole and Nan Oyl, and Olive's beau, Ham Gravy. Olive and Ham provided the comic strip's romantic moments: "Is that your nose or are you eating a cucumber?" In 1929, ten years after "Thimble Theatre" began, the Oyl family decided to go on a sea voyage. They needed a sailor to accompany them. Suddenly Castor Oyl spots a homely sailor with an unmistakable squint.

Castor: "Hey there! Are you a sailor?" Sailor: " 'Ja think I'm a cowboy?" The sailor's name was "Popeye," and the rest is history. "Thimble Theatre" is one of the few cases where a later tear sheet is more valuable than the debut episode. That particular 1929 "Thimble Theatre" is valued at $150 or more.

Winnie Winkle the Breadwinner. Winnie was the first career woman. Beginning in 1920, the series was originally drawn by Martin Branner. "Winnie Winkle the Breadwinner" is a favorite with many comic-strip buffs, particularly women. Branner always pictured Winnie in the latest fashions, so that, in its heyday, the comic strip was a real trend-setter. Women in northern Minnesota could tell what they were wearing that week in New York simply by scanning the latest "Winnie Winkle" episode. "Winnie Winkle" tear sheets of the 1920's vintage are usually sold in lots (as are her contemporaries "Tillie the Toiler" and "Etta Kett"). A dozen Winkles usually go for about $10.

Barney Google. The most popular comic strip feature of the 1920's was Billy DeBeck's "Barney Google." Though begun in 1919, the series really didn't get moving until 1922, when "Sparkplug" (Barney's horse) was worked into the strip. Although Sparkplug looked more like an overstuffed couch than a horse, Barney was always betting on him to win at the races — which Sparky never did. "Barney Google" was everyone's favorite; much of the strip's popularity doubtless rested on the fact that no matter how bad your day had been, you could be sure that Barney's would be worse! Take for instance the following lines from the popular 1924 song:

> *Barney Google with his goo-goo-googley eyes,*
> *Barney Google said his horse would win the prize.*
> *When the horse ran that day*
> *Sparkplug ran the other way!*
> *Barney Google with his goo-goo-googley eyes.*
>
> *Barney Google with his goo-goo-googley eyes,*
> *Barney Google tried to enter Paradise.*
> *When St. Peter saw his face*
> *He said "Go to the other place!"*
> *Barney Google with his goo-goo-googley eyes.* *

And you thought you had problems!

The American comic strip has been called art for the masses; certainly it is a totally original art form and particularly American. For more than eighty years, a legion of cartoonists have dedicated themselves to trying to make us laugh at ourselves and the things that go on around us. Their success can be measured in the longevity of their art form. The earliest of their works are now considered antiques — yet the medium remains as alive and vibrant today as ever. If you don't believe it, pick up a Sunday paper this week and see for yourself. □ □

Sheet Music

The glorious days of Tin Pan Alley

DURING the early years of this century nearly every parlor boasted a piano heaped with all the latest sheet music from Tin Pan Alley. Here families would gather to vocalize ballads, show tunes, rags, hot jazz and — oh, those novelties. Who today remembers such ditties as "Come Josephine in My Flying Machine" (1910), "I'm Forever Blowing Bubbles" (1919), "Kangaroo Hop" (1915) and "The Baboon Baby Dance" (1911)? Sheet-music collectors remember!

According to Kurt Baerg, past president and current treasurer of the National Sheet Music Society (1597 Fair Park Avenue, Los Angeles, CA 90041), sheet-music collecting is one of the fastest growing fields of Americana today. The NSMS has been rallying sheet-music collectors together for twenty years. The areas of interest are as varied as the backgrounds of the members themselves — particular ones include ragtime, blues, World War I songs, transportation songs (train, plane, boat, car), movie covers, Broadway musicals, or covers with pictures of famous per-

The Bing Crosby autograph on the sheet shown upper left confers real value on a sheet bought in a batch of otherwise unremarkable music.

Remembrances of Things Past/*Sheet Music*

sonalities such as Al Jolson, Eddie Cantor, and Sophie Tucker. For the $8 yearly dues, members of the Society receive a monthly newsletter and a directory putting them in touch with other members around the country.

The popularity of sheet music is easy to understand. Sheet music is readily collectable; whole boxes of it can often be picked up at auction for "a song" — or somewhere between $3 and $10. Even the more desirable individual sheets can be purchased usually for $5 or $10. An item priced at $30 or more is really "hot"! Measuring a constant 11 by 13 inches if published before 1918, or 9 by 12 inches for post-1918 music, the sheets stack conveniently, are easy to store, and most important, perhaps, make very attractive exhibits. Some collectors mount sheet covers in frames, others wallpaper entire rooms with them. A large part of the appeal of sheet music lies in the colorful covers; usually the more elaborate the cover, the more desirable the sheet, from a collecting standpoint. The E. T. Paull Music Company of West Forty-second Street in New York, in particular, turned out covers between 1900 and 1925 which are considered printed masterpieces. The songs themselves (many written by the company's own E. T. Paull) were rather undistinguished, including titles like "America Forever March," "Dawn of the Century" and "Lincoln Centennial March." Despite the fact that no E. T. Paull song ever became a "standard" (popular classic), the covers published by the company were so beautiful that collectors pay top prices ($15 to $25 or more) for sheets in very good condition.

There are other factors to consider when collecting sheet music. The cover may have been done by a noted artist, as many World War I song covers were, painted by the likes of Harrison Fisher, Howard Chandler Christy, and Norman Rockwell. The initial publication of a musical standard, such as "Sweet Adeline" (1903), "Let Me Call You Sweetheart" (1910), and "By the Light of the Silvery Moon" (1909), can fetch top prices, too. Short-lived songs performed by the famous entertainers portrayed on the covers, can score high sales: Al Jolson's "Where Did Robinson Crusoe Go with Friday on Saturday Night?" is a good example. And early compositions by soon-to-be-famous songsmiths are at a special premium. The sheet music for Irving Berlin's "Si's Been Drinking Cider" (1913) is difficult to find. George Gershwin's "Tee Oodle Um Bum Bo" (1919) and "Come to the Moon" (1919) may not measure up musically to his later "Rhapsody in Blue" and "I Got Rhythm," but in the field of sheet-music collecting, they're worth much more.

Because what appears on the cover of a piece of sheet music is often more important to collectors than the musical score inside, they have begun to establish the identities of the more prolific cover artists of the period. The names of many of these artists will likely forever remain unknown as over half of all song-sheet covers were unsigned. Yet even so, many artists left behind a partial key to their identities — sometimes just initials, as in the case of the artist who signed his work "R.S." Noted for his (or her) light and comical covers, he marked them only with these intitials coupled with his trademark of a rose. Albert Barbelle, on the other hand, is known to have produced a wide variety of covers distinctive for their haunting beauty during the 1920's. Covers by an artist named Starmer spanning the years from the 1890's to the 1940's, and the Traditional, Art Nouveau and Art Deco styles are very popular. Lovely covers in soft hues featuring beautiful women were the hallmark of portraitist Frederick S. Manning, who did work for Jerome H. Remick & Co. of New York.

Gene Buck is a name familiar to students of popular American music, but not for artwork. Gaining note in later years as a lyricist (for Ziegfeld's "Follies") and music industry executive, Buck began his career as an artist. Born in Detroit in 1885, he studied at the Detroit Art Academy, then entered the music field by landing a job as an art designer for Whitney and Warner, Detroit stationers who worked in conjunction with New York music publishers. When Remick of New York purchased Whitney and Warner, Buck was hired to design all the song covers published by the company. In 1911, Gene Buck turned to writing song lyrics and producing musical shows, going on to help discover Eddie Cantor, Will Rogers and Ed Wynn.

Also popular with sheet music collectors are "event songs," written to commemorate news of their time. The San Francisco earthquake prompted Helen Osborne and Walter Potter to pen "The Sweetheart That I Lost in Dear Old 'Frisco," a tearjerker self-described as "a beautiful song-story description of the Earthquake at San Francisco on the morning of April 18th, 1906." Twenty-one years later, Lindbergh's Atlantic crossing gave rise to "Lucky Lindy," "Charlie Boy (We Love You)," and a hundred other related songs. Advances in radio technology brought forth

Below: *Music to the extreme left and right was autographed for the author's collection by Benny Goodman and Guy Lombardo. Center left cover is an obscure song collectable due to its connection with Al Jolson (pictured). Center middle cover bears photographs of both Sophie Tucker and Harry Von Tilzer. Center right, "Dardanella," with lyrics by Fred Fisher, did so well that Fisher was able to start his own firm, publishing among others, the song shown on page 36, "Lookin' Out the Window."*

This patriotic World War I song would never get by the Surgeon General today. Harry Von Tilzer again.

"There's a Wireless Station Down in My Heart" (1914). The movies gave us "Mister Moving Picture Man" by Moriarty and Shannon in 1912. Even the up-and-coming new rival to sheet music was ironically celebrated by a New York company in 1914 when they published "They Start the Victrola (and Go Dancing Around the Floor)."

Typical of major collectors today is Dan McCall of 50 Grove Street, New York City. Mr. McCall, a member of the National Sheet Music Society, has accumulated one of the largest collections of sheet music in the country, a hobby that is of practical use in his career. Frequently touring the country as a professional banjoist, he's known in music circles as "Banjo Dan." As McCall explains it, "The reason I got into sheet music was simply because I wanted to play the old songs correctly." Because most musical standards have experienced lyrical and harmonic changes through the years, Mr. McCall started buying up early sheets seeking the original scores.

The collection now comprises over sixty thousand individual song sheets, all carefully arranged in categories. The walls of Dan McCall's living room are piled to the ceiling with filing boxes bearing such identifying labels as Automobiles, Flag Wavers, Money, Mammy and Mother, Girls' Names, States, Military, and Roses. The collection includes two hundred different songs about roses, alone. "We're in the Money" and "Brother, Can You Spare a Dime" are hits in the "money song" collection, which also contains non-moneymakers like "Two-Buck Tim from Timbuktu" and "Cohen Owes Me Ninety-Seven Dollars." The latter is a rare early Irving Berlin song wherein a man on his deathbed reminds his son to be sure and get that Ninety-Seven!

Sheet-music collectors specialize in many different ways — state songs (left) or Ireland (right), for example. Center sheet was written and published by E. T. Paull.

As for automobile songs, he has hundreds. People still remember "In My Merry Oldsmobile," but how about "The Little Ford That Rambled Right Along"?

Now they ran over glass and they ran over nails,
And then ran over pigs and puppy dog tails.
When she blows out a tire, just wrap it up with wire,
And the little Ford will ramble right along.

Then there is "Ray and His Chevrolet," "In a Hupmobile for Two," "In My Mercer Racing Car" — in fact, if you dig long enough you'll find that nearly every automobile manufacturer had a song written about his car.

Collectors find it more economical to buy music in large lots. If someone is breaking up an estate and disposing of things, there will often be a box of music. Rather than taking the time to sell each sheet for a dollar or two apiece, those handling the sale normally prefer to sell the box as a whole — for which they may realize $10-$15. If you are lucky, one sheet in the box may well be worth the whole $10!

In sorting out the music contained in such a box lot, collectors often find duplicates. This is where trading with other collectors proves beneficial. Many send out regular listings to trade-and-sell sheets. Collectors dealing with fellow buffs by mail find that condition has a lot to do with the salability of sheets. Anything described as mint has to look as if it just came off the press yesterday — it can't have a crease, a bend, a fold or a scuff. Ragged, badly torn, or marked-up sheet music is worthless to most collectors, unless, of course, it can be shown that the markings were notations put there by a famous musician or performer.

The first American song to sell a million copies of sheet music was a tune written by Charles K. Harris in 1892 called "After the Ball." From that point on, music publishing was big business. New York City quickly emerged as the capital of the music-publishing industry, with literally hundreds of music publishers issuing thousands of songs yearly from New York's "Tin Pan Alley." The term Tin Pan Alley first appeared in an early 1900's entertainment publication called the *Clipper*. The *Clipper* sent a reporter to a section of Twenty-eighth Street (where songwriters congregated) to put together a story about the nation's music trends. The tinkling of scores of tinny pianos which greeted him from the apartment buildings on Twenty-eighth Street reminded the reporter of the clanging of tin pans. The article that resulted was called "Down in Tin Pan Alley" and the name stuck.

At the time one of Tin Pan Alley's most prolific composers was a gentleman named Harry Von Tilzer. Before Irving Berlin became famous, Harry Von Tilzer was known as the King of Tin Pan Alley. His reign lasted from 1900 until World War I. Von Tilzer's first success came in 1898 when he teamed up with lyricist Andrew B. Sterling to write the sentimental ballad, "My Old New Hampshire Home:"

Now the sunshine lingers there,
And the roses bloom as fair,
In the wildwood where together we would roam.
In the village churchyard near
Sleeps the one I held so dear
On the hills of my old New Hampshire home.

Just the kind of lament that appealed to the melancholic tastes of the late nineteenth century, "My Old New Hampshire Home" became one of the biggest hits of the year. On the coattails of this success, Von Tilzer was able to form his own sheet-music publishing company, which introduced some of the hundreds of musical compositions he penned during his lifetime, including the immortal "Wait Till the Sun Shines, Nellie" and that durable choral number, "I Want a Girl Just Like the Girl That Married Dear Old Dad:"

I want a girl just like the girl that married dear old Dad.
She was a pearl and the only girl that Daddy ever had.
A good old-fashioned girl with heart so true,
One who loves nobody else but you.
I want a girl just like the girl that married dear old Dad.

Tin Pan Alley got a big boost from World War I, which inspired songs like George M. Cohan's "Over There" and Irving Berlin's "Oh! How I Hate to Get Up in the Morning." The Alley continued to flourish into the twenties as ragtime gave way to jazz. But by 1929 the motion pictures had learned to sing, and movie musicals began to lure some of the country's best songwriters away to the West Coast. During the thirties the top songs were coming out of Hollywood, and Tin Pan Alley was on the way out. In fact, if you visit Twenty-eighth Street today, you'll find it given over to wholesale florists.

As Dan McCall remarks, "Up until very recently nobody collected sheet music — it was a throwaway item. Everyone passed it by, including museums and libraries. But now they're catching on. I advise people who want to collect sheet music to start now. Everything is going to escalate. It's already happening, partly because of the publication of price guides — but mostly because it's interesting."

The motto of the National Sheet Music Society is "The story of a nation is told in its song." Almost every phase of America's history is mirrored in song. But along with meaningful songs, there were also plenty of nonsense ditties like the 1916 gem "Yaddie Kaddie, Kiddie Kaddie Koo:"

When the milkman comes around in the morning,
I say, mister, leave a pint or two.
He says Yaddie Kaddie Kiddie Koo.

When the landlord calls I'm always yawning,
He don't ever say the rent is due.
All he says is Yaddie Kaddie Koo.

Please tell me why they sing that silly thing?
Yaddie Kaddie Koo, love your daddy, do.
Minnie Poo, me love you.

That melody from Waikiki
Hasn't any sense until they commence
Yaddie Kaddie Kiddie Kaddie Koo. *

Now that was music! □ □

Remembrances of Things Past/*Sheet Music*

Amazing
Contraptions

Telephones

From Alexander to "Ma" Bell

"TO us, there is nothing on earth more beautiful than a rare walnut wall phone completely restored, with its polished wood glowing and gongs chiming," a collector of antique telephones told me recently. A surprising number of people are today actively collecting the forerunners of the Princess and paying some high prices for the prestige of owning an authentic piece from the early years of the telephone age. A 1908 Vought-Berger cherry crank wall set today will cost you at least $140; a more common Western-Electric white-oak wall model of the same year bears a price of $195. For those wanting to start out small, black enamel "candlestick" desk phones from the 1920's today go for $60-$125, although ambitious collectors are assembling their own sets from parts for half this cost. For the collector whose tastes are on a grander scale, a complete 1914 deluxe Stromberg-Carlson walnut phone booth with velvet seat cover and marble directory table could be yours for $1000-$1200.

These are just a few examples of the items advertised for sale in the national newsletter of the Antique Telephone Collectors Association (614 Main Street, LaCrosse, KS 67548). Formed in 1971, the association now boasts a membership spanning the nation, devoted to expounding "the historical importance of old telephones" and providing "a means of communication between telephone collectors." Ten times a year, the association issues a newsletter featuring articles on collecting, letters from association members, news of vintage telephone exhibits, and a convenient advertising section for members.

Dr. Francis Fellers of New Gloucester, Maine, a charter member of the association, has built up one of the most extraordinary collections in the country. Dr. Fellers, who holds the official title of Scientific Advisor for the association, has been interested in early telephones for over thirty years and collecting actively for the past fifteen. The doctor's collection comprises some 350 phones. These range from the rare 1877 Williams box phone (the first commercial telephone in the world) and 1882 Blake three-box phone to the common single-box magneto phones. Other prizes are hand-cranked wooden wall sets, candlestick-model desk sets, pre-1925 dial phones, pay phones, complete switchboards, and early directories. But telephone collecting is not for everyone — it can be a weighty business indeed. Dr. Fellers' collection includes a solid oak phone booth and a couple of very heavy old switchboards. Moral: If you don't have a strong back, stick to knickknacks, or specialize in the smaller telephone-related artifacts, such as telephone-replica candy containers, blue telephone-bell paperweights, toy tin telephones, phone advertisements on calendars, fans and so on. Francis

Clockwise from upper left: *Fiddle- and straightback wooden wall sets; original highboy pay phone made by the Gray Telephone Pay Station of Hartford, Ct.; carved desk phone with mounted "cobra" mouthpiece.*

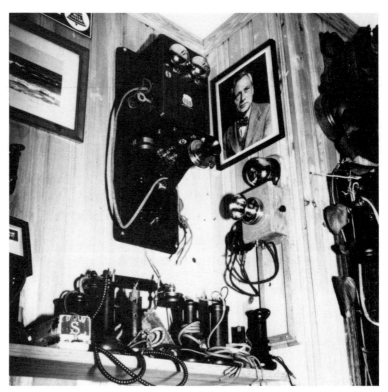

Right: *Center, top, American Electric "pony" type phone using a common battery. Below, early American cradle ("French") phone. Far right, intercom phone from Maine's Somerset Hotel, made by Plummer Co. of Worcester, Mass.*

Below: *The historic Williams telephone, first commercial phone in the world, a few hundred of which were made for Alexander Graham Bell in 1877-78 by electrician Charles Williams.*

Fellers has hunted up some fourteen hundred different early postcards which picture telephones.

Collectors of early telephone artifacts will tell you that the most difficult items to find today are those dating from 1877 to 1894, the initial years of development for the telephone. This period of great experimentation produced a large selection of diverse telephonic contraptions. The separate transmitter and receiver, the long-distance induction coil, and magneto generators were all evolved during this time. Wooden cabinets were a prominent feature of the wall phones of the era. These attractive cabinets today are among the most desired by collectors. White-oak cabinets are most common; the walnut and cherry models are much rarer. Completely restored cabinet sets dating from the 1880's to 1900 start at $150 today, even for the more ordinary models, if you can find one. But as one collector who had worked long and hard to restore an 1899 Ericsson single-box cherry wood phone told me, "The problem is that once you've worked on an old phone so long and so lovingly, you just can't part with it."

Wooden wall sets made in the late 1870's and 1880's consisted of five basic parts: the signal box on top (with its exterior crank and twin gongs), the backboard (sometimes called "straight-back" or "fiddle-back," depending on the shape), the transmitter (with mouthpiece) in the center, the receiver, usually mounted on the left side of the phone, and the battery box at the base. Rural phones had a larger battery box than city sets, since

extra power was needed to reach "Central" from the farm. When wet-cell batteries gave way to the more compact dry-cell batteries, beginning in 1895, the signal box and battery box on wall models were combined into one solid cabinet. By 1900 the reign of the huge two-boxer wall phones had ended.

Almost equally sought by collectors are the old desk sets known as "candlesticks," due to their shape. These were common accessories in offices all across the country from the time of their appearance in 1897 until the last candlesticks were phased out in 1928. Though most candlesticks were made of common metals with a black enamel finish, special porcelain, carved wood, brass, and silver models were also produced. Being special, these of course command higher prices. Candlestick phones were made by such companies as Kellogg, Ericsson, Leich, Whitman & Couch and others. One interesting candlestick model was made by the Deveau Company circa 1905. Called a multiple-line phone, it had an enlarged base and was in effect a forerunner of the modern intercom system. Along the base of surviving examples are a number of buttons with labels ranging from "kitchen" to "garage." This item currently sells for about $350-$400 in good condition.

Early phones did in fact come in all shapes and sizes, and often were made to resemble familiar items. One model popular during the early 1890's looked like a desk. Combination desk-phones were made by several of the early phone companies and were modeled after the set used by Alexander Graham Bell to

Above, left: In this rare old wooden model, either of the identical units hung below can serve as transmitter or receiver. Right: 1882 double-boxer magneto wall set, first of the sidewinder, or side-crank models.

make the first long-distance phone call from Chicago to New York at the 1892 Chicago World's Fair. A combination desk-phone I saw recently in a New Hampshire collection was made of beautifully carved cherry wood and sported a glass show window displaying the gongs and inner crankwork of the built-in apparatus. The mouthpiece was mounted above the desk's surface, and the receiver hung by the side. Any collector fortunate enough to locate such a phone today can expect to be able to resell it to the tune of $1500 or more.

Collectors for whom room space is not a problem often acquire switchboards, perhaps the largest and heaviest items in the field (although the earliest switchboards were rather compact). Ancestors of plug switchboards were "callboards," which looked rather like pinball machines. Callboards made in the late nineteenth century often had a dozen or more gongs, each of which

Right: *Ancestor of the plug switchboard was the callboard (center).*

Amazing Contraptions/*Telephones*

gave out different tones, so as to distinguish the different lines on the board. These were the first boards to be used in the operator's home; during peak telephone hours, their ringing gongs provided quite a rhapsody.

A popular collectable category in this field is telephone literature. This includes early books about the science of telephony when the invention was new and considered a wonderful novelty. Even those directories Ma Bell has been issuing over the years have begun gaining in value. A New York telephone book from the mid-1920's can easily fetch $20 to $25 from a collector today. The earliest directories dating back from the nineteenth century provided telephone users with helpful hints of phone etiquette, such as, "Gentlemen are asked to please not chew tobacco while using the telephone." The first telephone directory was a single sheet affair issued in Boston in 1878 by the Telephone Dis-

Left: *Center phone below is white porcelain on steel, probably made for a doctor's office; above is an unusual annunciator, or call box, dating from the 1880's and used in hotels or large houses to signal the staff. Telephone attachment permitted direct conversation. To right of the white phone are two dial Autophones made by Couch of Boston.*

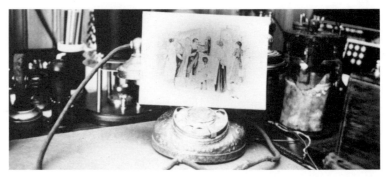

The drawing, "Neighborhood News," advertising a Kellogg wall telephone, is propped up on the silver-and-gold Kellogg cradle phone used on stage by Mary Martin in the musical, "South Pacific." Right, a "wet" battery.

patch Co. of 342 Washington Street. "The above company proposes, and is now prepared to establish direct telephonic communications between each and every business here in this city," the listing said. There were ninety-seven subscribers in that historic first directory, including two confectioners, seven druggists, four grocers, and a plow company. There were no phone numbers; calls were placed, the directory explained, "by communicating through the telephone, to a Central Office, that you desire to speak to Mr. A, B, or C. In an instant your communication is made direct and complete, and you can carry on your conversation."

Telephones themselves remain the most desirable items, if the number of want ads placed by collectors in antiques publications is any indication. There are certain points to keep in mind when purchasing an antique telephone. First of all, be sure that the cabinet of a wooden wall phone is not warped or cracked. Early phone design emphasized the beauty of the appliance as much as its ability to function, and thus modern collectors place a high value on a phone's appearance. If the telephone is in top condition, the transmitter, receiver and wiring should be free of cracks. The magneto crank should turn freely, but the gongs often will not chime unless the wiring is altered. In repairing early equipment, one resorts to reproduced replacement parts only after diligent search for original accessories has proven fruitless. Tracking down parts to restore phones is not quite the impossible task it once was inasmuch as contact between collectors has been greatly improved by the formation of groups such as the Antique Telephone Collectors Association.

Collectors of telephone memorabilia enjoy relating the stories behind items in their collections. Dick Violette of Contoocook, New Hampshire, tells a story about an original highboy pay phone he acquired a number of years ago, made by the Gray Telephone Pay Station Company of Hartford, Connecticut. William Gray patented the first coin-operated telephone on August 13, 1889, and was soon doing a brisk trade, garnering the early profits of what was to become an enormous business. "The phone in my collection was installed in Reed's Drug Store in Contoocook in 1898 and taken out of service in 1912. The phone could be fed nickels, dimes, quarters, half dollars, silver dollars, and that's not all. The drug store was next to a machinery shop which punched out waste slugs daily. Folks soon discovered that these fit nicely into the pay phone!" The disgruntled owner of the drug store had the phone taken out, and today it rests peacefully in the Violette collection. □ □

Musical Boxes

The magical world of mechanical music

Drum table musical box, circa 1899 —
one of less than a dozen manufactured.

THE mere mention of a musical box evokes the America of ninety to seventy-five years ago, when music boxes in the parlor were all the vogue. "Your mother, wife or daughter will appreciate a Christmas present so beautifully expressed as in the form of a Regina music box," one 1895 holiday ad read. "Perfect, refined, each note sent directly from heaven." For the most part superbly made, antique music boxes have not lost their appeal, and today are the subject of eager collecting interest despite some pretty high prices. These are not five-and-dime collectibles, but they cost considerably less than some furniture, antique automobiles or paintings. For example an Olympia table model disc-playing machine from the 1890's was recently offered for $2300 in restored and refinished condition. A Stella disc box, with ten 17½-inch discs and a storage drawer built into its golden oak case, sold for $2295. A very rare Nicole Frères cylinder box, with six revolving cylinders of operatic selections, was listed in a dealer's catalogue for $17,500, one of the highest prices ever quoted

Left: *Encore automated banjo, made in New England.* Right: *15½-inch, single-comb Reginaphone. In need of some cleaning and adjustment, this instrument still is valued at almost $2000.*

for a music box of any kind. But it is also possible to purchase an antique music box in playing condition for $300-$400.

The Musical Box Society International (Box 202, Route 3, Morgantown, IN 46160) has been bringing collectors of mechanical music together since 1949, and currently has about twenty-five hundred members. At its start, the society's original twenty-five members met in the home of a collector. Today it is literally an international organization, with members from all over the world. The society holds one national convention a year, usually in late September, in different parts of the United States on a rotating basis. There are five regional chapters, which also convene local meetings. These are the East Coast chapter, the Mid-America chapter, the Golden Gate chapter, the Nation's Capitol chapter, and the Pacific Northwest chapter. Regional chapters meet throughout the year, some every month, others four times a year, and these meetings are planned to be of interest to the beginning collector. The national society puts out a news bulletin (issued six times a year) and a technical journal (three times yearly). The bulletin contains newsy information about the hobby, meeting reports, information about new members, and advertisements. The technical journal covers the repair and restoration of machines, invaluable to the serious collector.

One member of the East Coast chapter is William Edgerton, of Darien, Connecticut. Mr. Edgerton runs a business called the Mechanical Music Center, Inc. (located at 25 Kings Highway, North, in Darien) and has been collecting music boxes for twenty years, although his interest in mechanical music goes back much further than that. "I grew up with a reproducing piano at home," Mr. Edgerton told me during my visit to his store. A reproducing piano, he explained, is a sophisticated player piano, with the capability of reproducing music with all of its intended expression. "They were electric and often styled as grand pianos," he said. This early introduction to mechanical music made a lasting impression on him, and about 1960 he began getting serious about collecting all kinds of music boxes. Early in his collecting, he had bought a cylinder music box in need of repairs at an antique shop for $60. He had it repaired, played it and liked it. The man who did the repair asked Edgerton if he'd part with it. He did, for $120, or

Below: *Regina musical grandfather's clock.*

Left: *15¾-inch Olympia Princess duplex disc box, with lid picture.*

twice what he had paid, and thought he had done very well, until he learned that the music box was very desirable due to its large cylinder. The man who bought it informed him that the machine could be sold immediately for $600 to $700. Today, the current value of that music box is about $4,000.

Mr. Edgerton said that shortly after this experience, he began to accumulate all kinds of mechanical musical instruments. "As many collectors do, I got to the point where my entire garage was filled with stuff. I just couldn't pass up something that I thought was a bargain." Joining the Musical Box Society International quickly put him in contact with other collectors. "I began to buy and sell instruments frequently and this developed into a part-time business," he said. During this period, Mr. Edgerton was running his own small publishing business, and decided to put out his own catalogue of mechanical musical items for sale. Finally, in the spring of 1977, he made the decision to sell his publishing business and turn what had begun as a hobby into a full-time business, buying and selling music boxes, player pianos, and orchestrions, as well as musical toys and novelties.

Walking through his showroom, the collector began to point out some of the particularly outstanding instruments. A Swiss-made music box he described as the rarest music box in the room. Most of the exterior of the case was inlaid with mother-of-pearl. "It came out of the third floor of a Brooklyn house yesterday." Another beautiful machine is a Regina, with a serpentine case and marvelous tone. It was priced at $3250. An Olympia Princess disc music box, with a stained glass picture under its lid, was tagged at $1550, while a 10-inch Symphonion music box with sixteen discs and a walnut case was more modestly priced at $695. "We really don't need a showroom," Mr. Edgerton remarked. "We could work totally out of a warehouse, as we sell very little to the walk-in traffic. The kind of person who comes here to buy is usually the serious collector who will go out of his way to stop here to see first-hand something he saw in our catalogue, to arrange the transfer of an item he has purchased, or to see what we have in stock."

Dealers in mechanical music say that they can always sell good-quality musical boxes, and both kinds of musical box are being sought by collectors today — cylinder machines, and the later disc music boxes. The cylinder music box was first developed in the late eighteenth century, but it enjoyed its greatest popularity in the years from 1860 to 1900. These cylinder machines consist of a pinned cylinder and a tuned metal comb with teeth of various lengths, usually mounted within a wooden cabinet (although some of the earliest were often to be found within snuff boxes or in the bases of mechanical dolls). Each of the teeth on the metal comb was designed to register a different note when struck by one of the thousands of pins found on the cylinder. During the second half of the nineteenth century, a vast variety of cylinder boxes was being produced. Cylinder music boxes were produced to play four, six, eight, ten, and twelve tunes. On early specimens, the cylinders were permanently placed within the cases and couldn't be removed, the selections being

Some musical novelties. Far left: *Automated animal orchestra "plays" different instruments.* Left: *A musical painting that also keeps the time.* Below: *A beautifully inlaid case houses this 17¼-inch Stella. Stella made these cases particularly for the English market.*

changed by automatic shifts within the boxes themselves. Thereafter, to expand the musical program, boxes with changeable cylinders were introduced.

Disc music boxes first appeared in the 1890's, and the most popular name was made in Rahway, New Jersey. Called Regina, "the Queen of Music Makers," this type of disc-playing machine offered a revolutionary innovation — changeable tunes. The perforated discs that replaced the old pinned cylinders made it possible for a family to play a whole library of different tunes on one Regina. Models could be purchased for anywhere between a few dollars for simple cabinet boxes, to thousands for the more elaborate upright machines which could play and change twelve discs in succession. Although Regina was the first to popularize the disc music box in this country, the company quickly had its share of competitors. A firm in nearby Jersey City, New Jersey, the Otto Manufacturing Company, produced two fast-selling models, the Olympia and the Criterion. Among the other names then on the market were Stella, Polyphon, Miraphone, Symphonion, Fortuna, and Brittania.

Music boxes were originally sold in music stores. The buyer would receive a small selection of discs with the machine at no additional cost, and could then continue to purchase more through their catalogue. Regina's disc catalogue from the mid-1890's offered over a thousand discs at 60¢ each, including selections from popular musicals, Sousa's marches, grand and comic operas, as well as assorted waltzes and popular tunes of the day. Collectors say it is still possible on occasion to find a box of old music-box discs at flea markets, yard sales, and tucked away in the corners of junk shops. Music-box discs were produced in a wide range of sizes, with the most common being the 15½-inch Regina discs. Dealers say they have no difficulty in keeping discs of this size constantly in stock, as they were heavily mass-produced. Some of the more unusual sizes, on the other hand, are very hard to find. For their thirty-odd different models, Regina, for example, manufactured discs ranging from 8½ inches in diameter to 32 inches across. Discs in either one of these extremes are difficult to acquire today, but it is even more difficult to find discs for instruments that sold in relatively small quantities.

From the start, the music-box and the phonograph industries were rivals. Their competitiveness stemmed from the fact that they were basically pursuing the same market, the home entertainment field. There were parallels between the two industries.

Both music boxes and phonographs made the transition from cylinders to discs. Both appealed to the ear. Yet, as time went on, phonograph manufacturers were able to mass produce their records more rapidly and less expensively than the music-box companies could produce their discs. Each disc had to be individually designed. The largest discs might contain as many as four thousand microscopic holes, from which the tinkling rhapsodies were produced. The problem which faced music-box producers was that, even though during their peak period they offered thousands of different discs, they were limited by the fact that discs played a tuned steel comb. No further variation was possible. The phonograph, meanwhile, had no such limitation. Its selection could include a band, an opera singer, somebody reading poetry, or even a political speech.

It was only a matter of time before the phonograph would win out. Regina, in fact, tried to fight this off by introducing for a short period at the end of its life a machine called the Reginaphone, which could play both music box discs and 78 RPM records. The cases were usually mahogany and quite attractive. Reginaphones complete with all parts are scarce, and when offered for public sale, the asking price is often over $3000!

By 1910, Victorian quaintness was fast giving way to ragtime, jazz, and the like. The music-box companies just could not compete. The last of the big music-box producers to hold out, Regina, finally went bankrupt. (Today a successor makes a vacuum cleaner known as the Regina electric broom.) A number of years ago, the Regina music-box factory records were acquired by a collector and microfilmed. Copies were supplied to the Musical Box Society International, so that collectors can inquire and, for a nominal fee, find out from its serial number when their particular machine was made and to whom it was shipped.

Collector-dealer William Edgerton believes that the best way for someone who may be interested in entering the field of mechanical music to find out about the hobby is to talk with a collector. "Talking with a collector will help the beginner to get the basic information he needs and the encouragement to read into the subject," he said. He suggests one book in particular for reading and reference: the *Encyclopedia of Automatic Musical Instruments* by Q. David Bowers, published by the Vestal Press in New York in 1972. "It is the definitive work on all forms of mechanical music, including music boxes." He also suggests membership in the Musical Box Society International, "which puts you in touch with people all around the world who share your interest."

For a few short years, the music box was truly the marvel of home entertainment. A Regina ad in the June 1896 issue of *Munsey's Magazine* told Americans that "musical people wonder at its brilliancy of tone and artistic effects. It is unrivalled as a social entertainer. Never needs tuning, is always ready to play and will last a lifetime. A constant delight to any home." On the very same page appeared a much smaller ad for the infant Columbia Phonograph Company, reading "It plays, sings and talks!" A claim that subsequently proved hard to beat. □ □

Phonographs and Record Makers

. . . the winner and still champ . . .

B EN Thacher of Massachusetts first began collecting early phonographs and records about seventeen years ago. As a professional magician and puppeteer, he became interested in acquiring recordings of the early entertainers of the American stage. Because some were on cylinders, he needed a cylinder machine to play them. That was just the start, as it turned out, Mr. Thacher remembers. He subsequently began picking up other early machines as he added to his record collection — "all kinds of phonographs — cylinders, disc players, the early machines with the morning-glory horns, Victrolas, whatever."

Today, Ben Thacher owns what is recognized as one of the finest collections of early phonographs and records in the country, displayed in his museum, "Old Sound," located on Route 134, in East Dennis, Massachusetts. The collection includes over two hundred "talking machines" of all shapes and sizes and over thirty thousand recordings. "It really is incredible the variety of things that have been recorded in this country down through the years," Mr. Thacher said. "Everything from the cry of an injured rabbit to grand opera."

Phonograph and record collecting has seen a considerable expansion over recent years. The hobby received a big boost in 1977 with the centennial of the invention of the phonograph. Prof. Allen Koenigsberg, publisher of *The Antique Phonograph Monthly,* pointed out that commemorative stamps were issued in many countries — there was even a stamp issued in India!

Mr. Koenigsberg has been collecting since 1966, when he saw his first antique phonograph — an early Edison machine with a

Reproducing Speech

large morning-glory horn. Also about this time, he discovered an original 1907 trade catalogue illustrating all the Edison phonographs then available, an invaluable source for collectors. It proved so useful, in fact, that a few years later he had a thousand copies of the catalogue printed and sold them for two dollars each. This put him in contact with other collectors around the country, and soon a chain of correspondence was formed. He published another book listing all the Edison cylinders made up until 1912, and finally *The Antique Phonograph Monthly,* beginning in 1973.

Prof. Koenigsberg's readers are the closest there is to a national organization at the moment. He added that a national convention in the near future is being considered, to see if some formal organization could be developed. His journal features how-to articles on machine repair and maintenance, stories about the early companies, current news of interest to collectors, and an advertising section including ads from all around the country. The publication currently reaches fifteen hundred subscribers. For more information, write *The Antique Phonograph Monthly,* 650 Ocean Avenue, Brooklyn, NY 11226.

As a collector, Allen Koenigsberg specializes in pre-1900 Edison cylinder machines and recordings. Discoveries in this field are increasingly few and far between, as these machines are getting very difficult to find. Edison Home model cylinder machines are now averaging from $250 to $300, while Edison Gem cylinder machines exceed $275.

Koenigsberg's collection currently includes about five thousand cylinder recordings. A big problem with cylinder collecting is storage. Flat-disc recordings can be conveniently stored in "bins," but cylinders are usually kept on pegs. "Companies used to manufacture peg cabinets for storing cylinder records, and these are in growing demand among collectors," Prof. Koenigsberg said. "Newly manufactured peg cabinets are now available, however, and are proving to be very helpful." Collectors also strive to acquire the colorful boxes that originally contained the records. These were felt-lined cardboard boxes which are just the thing for keeping recordings in tip-top condition, although excessive moisture is still to be avoided. Condition is very important in cylinder collecting. The earliest cylinders were made of brown wax and are very fragile. Later cylinders were more durable, being made of celluloid (Edison, Lambert, Indestructible, etc.).

When Edison first invented the phonograph in 1877, he saw it more as an office accessory — a machine for taking dictation — rather than the entertainment medium it was to become. But office use was only one of many applications. The new machine turned out to be the wonder of the age. The phonograph first appeared in the American home and office during the winter of 1889. That Christmas, shoppers were introduced to an odd-looking contraption which, it was claimed, would reproduce the human voice. Publications of the era displayed flashy announcements that "The Marvel of the Phonograph Has Come!," assuring that it "Only asks a hearing." Machines were at first leased, then sold outright.

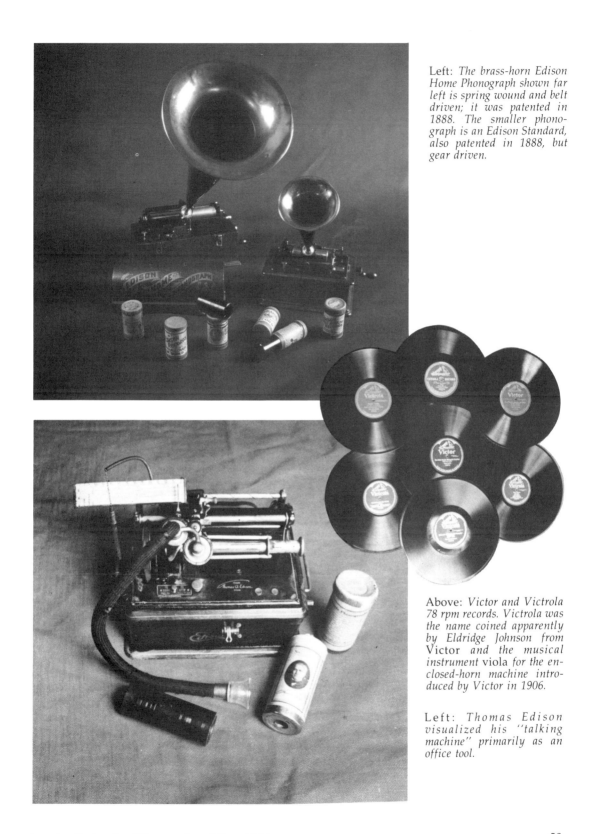

Left: *The brass-horn Edison Home Phonograph shown far left is spring wound and belt driven; it was patented in 1888. The smaller phonograph is an Edison Standard, also patented in 1888, but gear driven.*

Above: *Victor and Victrola 78 rpm records. Victrola was the name coined apparently by Eldridge Johnson from Victor and the musical instrument viola for the enclosed-horn machine introduced by Victor in 1906.*

Left: *Thomas Edison visualized his "talking machine" primarily as an office tool.*

The possibility of recording the human voice attracted many an entrepreneur, and independent companies sprang up all over like mushrooms in the late 1890's. Advertisements for machines now long forgotten, like the Polyphone (made by the Talking Machine Company of Chicago) and the Columbia Graphophone (pride of the Eastern Talking Machine Company), filled the magazines of the period. Everyone wanted to get into the exciting new field of phonographs and phonograph records. In the nineties many phonograph businesses had their start in a garage or storehouse. Production was slow, and only a small selection of recordings could be offered. In 1896, Thomas Edison finally became persuaded of the entertainment potential of his invention, and formed the National Phonograph Company (later to be known as Thomas A. Edison, Inc.), which made and distributed cylinder recordings of bands, novelty narratives, and a dash of the classics.

Edison's biggest competition soon came from a German immigrant, Emile Berliner, who had devised a method of recording on discs instead of cylinders. Berliner formed the Berliner Gramophone Company in 1895 and began manufacturing the first flat-disc recordings offered for home use. Berliner's method required the recording of only one master copy of each selection, from which master dozens of "biscuits" could be pressed. By contrast, Edison's method called for the musician to sing into the recording horn over and over again as each cylinder was being recorded. The process was slow and the repetitions exhausted singer and band, so that cylinder recordings were often hoarse and off-key. Only after 1902 were cylinders made from molds.

For a number of years to follow, competition between the Berliner and Edison companies was strong, and both spent enormous sums on advertising. Finally, in 1902, Berliner sold out and joined forces with Eldridge Johnson, who had produced the first spring-driven motor gramophones, thus creating uniform speed throughout the recording, to form The Victor Talking Machine Company. The trademark of the new firm was a reproduction of English artist Francis Barraud's painting, "His Master's Voice." The dog and horn soon appeared on each record issued by the company and, in time, became one of the most famous American trademarks. The disc industry (which included Columbia, as well) soon rivalled and surpassed Edison's enterprise.

Many of the earlier Victor disc machines now sell for $300 to $400. In 1976, a rare coin-operated upright oak cabinet disc phonograph, made by the Daily Concertphone Company of Chicago in the 1920's was offered for sale in *The Antique Phonograph Monthly* at a price of $1750. The machine, which played on dimes, featured a heavy glass top and four turntables, each of which rises to meet a mounted, pivoted acoustic tone arm.

Thomas Edison stood by his original idea of the cylinder method almost to the bitter end. In 1912, he relented and issued a flat-disc line called Edison Diamond Disc Re-creation. His records were nearly a quarter inch thick, and were originally priced at $2 each. They could only be played on Edison diamond-stylus machines, recorded as they were vertically (along the bottom of the grooves), instead of by the lateral vibration method (in the groove's walls). For this reason, Edison discs, although impressive-looking, are not very popular with today's collectors. It's just too difficult to find modern machines that can play them. When Thomas Edison retired from the phonograph business in 1929, the company, still bearing the great inventor's name, once again concentrated on producing dictating machines.

Recordings left behind by the myriad other short-lived firms top collectors' lists today. A Berliner employee, Frank Seaman, broke away in 1899 to form his own disc recording company, Universal Talking Machine Co., which made Zonophone machines and records. Zonophone did quite well, but Berliner threatened to sue for patent violations, and in 1903 Seaman sold out to Victor. Zonophone records without paper labels are now priced somewhere between $5 and $12 each. (Prior to 1900, disc records were identified by words engraved in the shellac.)

Until 1908, all phonograph records were generally recorded on one side only. Then, via a large, double-page ad in the November 21, 1908 issue of *The Saturday Evening Post,* Columbia Records announced that double-sided records had come at last. (An earlier attempt to launch double-sided records in 1904 had failed.) Other companies followed, and "two records for the price of one" eventually won wide public approval.

For the nostalgic, early phonograph records bring to life the music and humor of a vanished era, told and sung by those who lived it. For the collector, they represent the potential thrill of discovery, the chance of stumbling upon pure gems like the disc recorded by Thomas Edison in 1918, commending the heroism of America's doughboys during World War I and titled "Let Us Not Forget," the speech by Teddy Roosevelt to the Boy Scouts of America recorded in 1912, or Enrico Caruso's "Pagliacci," recorded during his first visit to the Victor laboratories in New York on February 1, 1904.

Although many recordings have survived, many were carelessly broken or lost altogether. The puzzle of the Bettini records still baffles collectors.

As early as 1889, Gianni Bettini, a name in society circles of the time, became interested in the new talking machines. Not satisfied by buying a phonograph and recordings, he sought to record the voices of his friends for their entertainment and his own. Bettini's list of friends consisted of a dazzling assembly of the era's best known celebrities, and his records, made in the famous Sherwood Studio building on the corner of Fifty-seventh Street and Sixth Avenue in New York, surely constituted the most priceless collection of recordings ever made. It is quite certain that Bettini recorded Sarah Bernhardt's famous voice, and that another recording, made in December 1893, presented an amusing conversation between Nellie Melba and Mark Twain. Many personalities of the Metropolitan Opera who graced Bettini's phonograph records were never to be recorded again. It has been rumored for years among collectors that Pope Leo XIII and Queen Victoria actually recorded their voices on cylinders for Bet-

This beautiful example of a concealed-horn phonograph cabinet is extravagantly inlaid with mother-of-pearl.

Below, left: *The germ of the phonograph idea scrawled on a page from Edison's notebook.* Below, right: *Early newspaper advertisement.*

THE EDISON
PHONOGRAPH

Edison Phonographs are clearer, louder, better made and better finished than any other talking machines. A moment's inspection, and a *comparison* by using the *same record* on all machines, proves this positively.

"HOME" $30.

Therefore, if you want to enjoy your talking machine, insist on getting a genuine Edison Phonograph.

tini. (The Leo XIII cylinder was released by Columbia and has also turned up in a disc.)

In 1895, Bettini began selling his recordings on a small scale, for $2 to $6 a cylinder. This price never was competitive, as other companies were selling cylinders for as little as 50¢ each. The fate of the bulk of Bettini's valuable recordings is still a mystery, although a large collection stored in a French warehouse is known to have been destroyed during an air-raid in 1940. If ever located, Bettini cylinders could be worth a substantial fortune to a lucky collector. Perhaps cylinders bearing the voices of Mark Twain or Benjamin Harrison are hiding in some reader's attic at this moment. The brown Bettini cylinders are very difficult to identify.

Shortly after recounting the story of Gianni Bettini in *Yankee* Magazine a few years ago, I received an interesting letter from Mr. Nathaniel H. Freeman of New York City, who wrote: "I knew Mr. Bettini in his waning years, a fine, elegant gentleman. At that time, 1938, he had a two-room suite of offices at 67 West Forty-fourth Street. The rooms were piled ceiling high with his accumulation of materials. You wonder what happened to his material. Well, some months later, I dropped by his office. It was closed. I then sought out the superintendent, who informed me that Mr. Bettini had died. I asked him what has happened to all the material stacked in his office. His reply: 'Oh, that stuff? We threw it all in the furnace.' "

Today's collectors hope to preserve for posterity the machines and voices of those who came before. "We have been lucky enough to gain access to the early files of recording companies," said Allen Koenigsberg, of *The Antique Phonograph Monthly.* "Most present-day descendants of the early firms seem primarily interested in one thing," he said " — selling records, but they do allow us to look through their archives. Our research has turned up information important to collectors in dating certain machines and recordings."

Most phonograph collectors will tell you there is more than merely the dollar value involved in their interest. (The vast majority of 78 rpm recordings from the Teens and Twenties can still be picked up at second-hand stores and flea markets for well under a dollar.) Living history in sound, records bring us the voices of another era, just as they were in their own time. Nostalgia perhaps, time machine indeed! ☐ ☐

Photographica

Cameras and everything remotely connected with them

The two Wollensack lenses on this 5- by 7-inch glass-plate, stereo-view camera made in 1910 by the Corona View Corporation are spaced to approximate the distance between human eyes. Also shown are stereograph cards and a viewer.

"**Y**OU press the button, we do the rest" were the words that introduced the Kodak box camera to America in the year 1888. "Anybody who can wind a watch can use the Kodak Camera," an ad for the history-making product of the Eastman Dry Plate and Film Company of Rochester announced. "No tripod is required, no focusing, no adjustment whatsoever — simply point the camera and press the button."

Today the Kodak box camera, as well as a cavalcade of other early camera-related items, detective cameras, the stereopticon, the Brownies, and all the rest make up the popular field of "photographica." Although photographica covers practically everything that is even remotely connected with the field of photography and its advancement (from original glass wet-plate negatives to weighty journals on the science of photography), it is the cameras that attract the greatest attention among buffs. Their interests go all the way from the primitive gadgets predating actual photography, such as the camera obscura, to the highly prized 35-millimeter cameras produced just prior to World War II. In the field of camera collecting, age does not necessarily dictate value. Some of the cameras of the 1930's, the early Leicas, for example, are valued at as much as $20,000, while the common folding cameras from the 1920's often may be obtained for no more than $15-$20.

Thom Hindle of Dover, New Hampshire, has been collecting photographica for fifteen years. As one of the first serious collectors in the field, he was one of the twenty collectors featured in George Gilbert's book, *Collecting Photographica*. A 1974 article featuring Mr. Hindle and his cameras in *Yankee* magazine evoked correspondence that greatly expanded his collection. Today Mr. Hindle teaches and lectures on photography in the Dover area, and is in the process of converting an old barn into a studio. Here he hopes to house a permanent display of antique cameras and equipment.

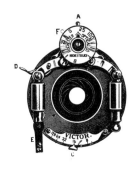

Mr. Hindle, like many other early camera buffs, is a member of the Photographic Historical Society of America (Box 71, Waltham Station, MA 02154). The many local and regional groups for collectors that exist around the country are in one way or another associated with the society. The Photographic Historical Society publishes its own periodical, *The North Light,* which

Stereograph cards from the author's collection show the United States Capitol (some time ago!) and "Maj. Gen. Jeff. C. Davis."

covers many different categories of photographica. A recent issue featured, for example, the art of collecting Leica cameras.

Thom Hindle's collection, like the field of photographica itself, is ever-changing. "At first I collected anything I could get my hands on associated with photography," he explained. "I gradually began to concentrate exclusively on collecting pre-1900 cameras and related items." At one point his collection included over a thousand cameras. "Most recently I began trading and selling these as I've become more interested in acquiring camera novelties. These are today considered among the most desirable items of photographica." One novelty in his collection is the Expo Watch Camera, a miniature camera introduced in 1905 and made to resemble a pocket watch. The camera was designed to hold a twenty-exposure film cartridge slightly smaller than 16 millimeters, and the lens was hidden in the winding stem. Quite rare today, such cameras are worth $125 or more if in "complete" condition.

Above: Camera-shaped candy container valued at $175. Below, left: Leica A (top) and miniature 1905 Expo camera (bottom) shaped like a pocket watch. Original box, view finder and film. Below, right: 1909 Conley folding camera, Sears & Roebuck's medium-quality line.

Also in the Hindle collection are cameras designed to look like whiskey flasks, a candy container shaped like a camera (valued at $175!), figurines with cameras, and other oddities of this kind, along with sheet music whose covers or lyrics feature cameras, vintage postcards picturing cameras, and a large collection of books on photography dating back over a century, including copies of *Humphrey's Journal*, one of the first continuously-run publications on photography. An 1876 Praktinascope caught my eye. This ingenious circular contraption resembling the base of a

hat box was a forerunner of the motion picture. A series of revolving cartoons are reflected on a group of centrally mounted mirrors, producing the illusion of a moving image when whirled.

Mr. Hindle sometimes puts his antique cameras to use, and is currently taking pictures with a 1901 panoramic camera. "The craftsmanship of the early cameras was really far superior to what we have today," he believes. However, it is difficult today to acquire film for the early cameras, even for those dating back only thirty years or so. "As these cameras became obsolete, companies ceased to produce film for them," he explained.

Camera collecting has changed markedly in recent years because of the increased publicity accorded the hobby by books and magazine articles on the subject, leading many people to seek out their old cameras and put them up for sale. The market was flooded with the more common antique cameras — folding Kodaks, to give one example. Nevertheless, the publicity has had a beneficial effect, bringing, as it has, some extremely rare items hidden for years to light and thereby adding to the understanding of the development of photography in this country.

The concept of the camera itself was known as early as the eleventh century, with the popular camera obscura. This was simply a box with a mirror and lens by means of which a small reproduction of a scene could be projected onto a surface. In Arabia, sheiks reportedly would set up camera obscuras inside their tents to amuse friends by "magically" projecting the desert scene outside onto a small table within. The device was also used for centuries by artists as a tool for producing scaled-down reproductions of original works of art. The history of modern photography, however, starts in 1839, when Louis Jacques Mande Daguerre, a Paris designer, developed the world's first practical process for producing photographic images.

Throughout the late eighteenth and early nineteenth centuries, glassmakers and chemists had been tinkering with the notion of permanently "fixing" the miniature scenes projected by the camera obscura on a light-sensitive surface. In 1839, the daguerreotype was born, when, using polished silver-covered copper plates made light-sensitive by being treated with iodine fumes, Daguerre realized the dream of the centuries. The news did not take long to reach America. In February of 1840, the *New York Mirror* described the first American exhibit of "this new and interesting art" based on the principles of Daguerre.

Early cameras of this period are rare, mainly because they were produced in limited numbers; camera design was constantly being altered as new improvements were discovered. Daguerre's camera was very simple — little more than a wooden box made with adjustable sections used to focus the mounted lens. There was no shutter. A cap placed over the lens was uncovered to register the image on the light-sensitive metal plate within the camera itself. Daguerreian cameras used no negatives and produced only one picture at a time. The French camera was quickly outmoded by the introduction by William Henry Fox Talbot of England of the negative-positive process of photography in the

Below: *Magic lantern, forebear of modern slide projectors. The oil lamp projected hand-painted glass slides, usually designed to entertain children. This one was made in Germany in the late 19th century.*

1840's, which made it possible to procure innumerable prints from a single exposure. The next stage in photography was reached with the discovery of the wet-plate process in the early 1850's; this method of photography prevailed for the next thirty years. Cameras of this era, as well as those which preceded them, are very rare and often worth thousands of dollars. Condition is very important in affixing value to these "museum pieces."

George Eastman's famous Kodak box camera and its transparent and flexible celluloid film made it possible for amateurs to take up photography, hitherto a field limited to professional studio and traveling photographers. The introduction of the Kodak box camera in the 1880's dramatically changed the situation. Photography for the masses had arrived. The new flexible film was eminently portable. "A picturesque diary of your trip to the mountains, or the seashore, may be obtained without trouble," an 1888 ad told Americans. Each Kodak camera was loaded with a film roll of one hundred exposures. To develop the film, the user returned the entire camera to Kodak, receiving back a reloaded camera and a stack of circular prints. In 1974 an original 1888 model priced for $500. More recent estimates see the value at nearly double that figure.

George Eastman, who prior to 1880 had been a bank clerk in New York, quickly saw to it that his new Kodak would lead all other makes in the field of amateur photography. When a Boston-based company came out in 1892 with a camera called the Bull's Eye, featuring a small red window through which the user could see the consecutive numbers as the film was advanced, Eastman began taking steps to acquire a license to use the idea on his Kodak box cameras. In 1895 he ended up buying the Boston Camera Company and the patent for the numbered film advancement system. Bull's Eye cameras from the early 1890's sell for $40-$60.

During the nineteenth century there were a great many photographic innovations. Stereopticons, invented in the 1830's, were one of the most ingenious. Stereographs captured the world as no other medium could, bringing the grandeur of the Colorado Rockies or the Florida Everglades right into your nineteenth century parlor.

Clear, vivid, three-dimensional and accurate in every detail, stereograph views are favorites with collectors and still immediately transport the modern-day viewer through both time and space to the very spot at which the camera was situated seventy-five to a hundred years ago or more. Although a great many singular view cards are still available, complete sets are becoming scarce. Those that do turn up usually command high prices. A complete ten-card set documenting the Chicago Fire of 1871 was once available for $1.50. Today this set brings in excess of $60. A basic rule of thumb for stereoview collectors, is that the historical importance of the event pictured is more important to the value of the card than is its age. Stereographs of the dedication ceremonies for the Statue of Liberty in 1886 are worth three times what views showing the opening of the Brooklyn Bridge in 1883 are.

Above, left: *Rare S-wing multiple camera produces 15 gem photos on one plate.* Above, right: *Newspaper photographers favored the Graflex cameras above — 3A (1903) and Series B (1925).*

Above, left: *A pre-motion picture optical toy, the Praktinascope is a museum piece today.* Above, right: *The Kombi miniature camera was first introduced at the 1893 Columbian Exposition.*

Above, left: *Original Boston Bullseye — a very rare wooden model.* Above, right: *Darkroom items add interest to a collection.*

Right: *The second version of the original one-dollar Brownie introduced by Eastman Kodak the summer of 1900.*

The viewers, in good condition, today sell for anywhere from about $20 for the cheapest, hand-held models produced by Sears and Roebuck and Montgomery Ward in the teens and twenties all the way to $200 for the French-made Gaumont parlor viewer, which stored twenty stereo cards and had a drop-feed mechanism.

A surprising number of twentieth century cameras have already become collectibles. In fact, some of the most expensive items in the field of photographica are certain 35-millimeter cameras produced in the twenties and thirties. Initially designed for motion-picture cameras, 35-millimeter film was first successfully used in cameras for still photography by the German company, Leica. The Leica Model A was first introduced in Europe in 1925, but it would be another decade or more before 35-millimeter cameras came into wide acceptance in America. Kodak didn't introduce the Kodak Ektra, its first 35-millimeter camera, until 1940.

Also collected, though not as valuable, are the single-lens and twin-lens reflex cameras made between 1900 and 1940. Twin-lens cameras employ two lenses, one on top for framing and focusing the picture, coupled with another lens beneath which actually conducts the light to the film. Single-lens reflex cameras use a system of mirrors that reflect the image for focusing through the same lens that conducts light to the film. The Graflex, which first appeared in 1903, was the leader of the American models. Early models in top condition sell for $150 or more.

Cameras through the years have been made in all shapes and sizes. They have been hidden in watches, stickpins, and even in the crowns of canes. To camera buffs, collecting gives a chance to own the sometimes unusual gadgets our great-grandparents used to preserve the images of each other.

A few years ago I found a cardboard-mounted circular print obviously taken with an early box camera. Pictured was an elderly man with a long flowing moustache, seated on a bicycle. On the back of the photograph was written, "Uncle Henry and his bicycle, Sept. 1895." Was the bicycle a recent gift to Uncle Henry, or was he a seasoned wheeler? Alas, we'll never know, because Uncle Henry is long gone from this world, and his bicycle is probably in a museum somewhere. But one sunny day eighty-five years ago, somebody thought this colorful character worth remembering, pointed the camera in his direction and pushed the button. His photograph survives. ☐ ☐

Section 3

Red Letter Days

Christmas Year 'Round

Santa Claus and all the trappings

Santa Claus as conceived by Theodore C. Boyd (above, with mouse-sized reindeer) and by Thomas Nast (right, exuding good cheer, and below, hard at work). Santa's popularity before the Civil War was such that he even appeared on a series of $5 bills in 1858, printed by Rawdon, Wright, Hatch, and Edson, a New York bank-note firm. Needless to say, these bills are very rare today; one can be seen in the museum in Santa Claus, Indiana.

REPRESENTING the most sentimental time of the year, Christmas items are naturals as nostalgia-provoking collectibles. We all collect Christmas in one way or another, whether it be treasuring a favorite family Christmas ornament, saving ribbon or wrapping, or keeping old Christmas cards in a shoebox. Our great-grandparents left us a rich heritage of old-time Yuletide mementos — a handmade ornament bearing the message "Merry Christmas, Phoebe, 1892;" a copy of *The Night Before Christmas* inscribed "From Auntie Sarah, December 1886;" a colorful holiday postcard dated December 22, 1903, reading simply "Will be arriving on the 6:05 —" evocative souvenirs of Christmases past.

Today such items are actively collected by Christmas buffs, who eagerly hunt for a particular Christmas-tree ornament or Santa Claus card. Christmas collecting encompasses a wide variety of items — figural glass ornaments, Santa postcards, books, advertising cards, various types of candle clips and glass holders, paper and papier-mâché ornaments, wax, tin and celluloid decorations, garlands, and even Christmas wrapping paper.

A very special and often quite expensive area of Christmas collecting is that of early ornaments. Most desirable are glass ornaments made in Europe in the nineteenth and early twentieth centuries. (Ornament production in this country is relatively new.) The first glass Christmas-tree ornaments manufactured for commercial trade were produced in 1848 in the German village of Lauscha, which was to become the Christmas-ornament capital of the world. The American chain-store magnate F.W. Woolworth imported tens of thousands of ornaments each year from Lauscha for his five-and-dime stores across the country. Germany had little competition in the production of ornaments until 1925, when Japan entered the market. When hostilities broke out between these countries and the United States, Americans found themselves cut off from their supply of Christmas ornaments. The Woolworth Company approached Corning Glass Works of Corning, New York, to fill the depleted supply. These were the first commercial Christmas ornaments made in this country.

Early German ornaments are presently fetching fantastic prices among collectors. It is not uncommon for some of the more intricate examples from the nineteenth century (figurines of angels, reindeer, and St. Nicholas) to command $75 to $150 or more. But don't expect to come upon these delicate gems easily. One collector who concentrates on acquiring interesting and valuable Christmas tree ornaments is Bette Pallos, of La Crescenta, California. "At first I thought I had a corner on the market, with little competition," Mrs. Pallos said. "But the more involved I became, the more aware I was that there were many others doing the same thing." Indeed, some collectors may search for years before securing a desired ornament for their collection.

Less expensive are Victorian paper decorations — a set of fifteen of these delightful fancies recently sold for $25. Even Christmas-tree light bulbs are collected, particularly those formed as images, popular during the 1930's and 1940's. Recently a clown-

Below: *Directions for making a Santa Claus by decking an "ordinary doll," with pine cones, flax, fur and moss.* Harper's Weekly, *1867.*

SANTA CLAUS.

DIRECTIONS FOR MAKING SANTA CLAUS.—Take five large pine cones, two for the arms, two for the legs, and one for the body; glue them together, and wind them round with wire. Cut the hands out of wood, set them on a block, sharpen the upper ends, and insert them in holes bored in the legs. Glue the head and hands of an ordinary jointed doll on the body and arms; make the beard and hair of flax, and fit a fur cap on the head. Put a girdle of dried moss round the waist, to conceal the wire, and a knit tippet on the neck. Fasten a pasteboard basket, filled with candies and toys, on the back; throw a netted bag, with nuts and lady-apples, over one shoulder; and put a miniature Christmas-tree in one hand, and a nut-cracker and switch in the other.

Santas from the Blanchard Collection. Top: Rare old Santa circa 1870. Bottom: Ceramic sleeping Santa is a coin bank.

shaped bulb brought $18, a puss-in-boots, $60. Look for these items at auctions, flea markets, yard sales, and friends' attics.

Many Yuletide collectibles — books, cards, toys, and prints — feature the grand old man of the North Pole. And collecting Santa Claus figures of all sizes and guises is also a popular aim. It is hard to believe that the American concept of St. Nick is only a little over 150 years old, born on December 23, 1823, in the pages of a rather obscure upstate New York weekly called the *Troy Sentinel.* This was the issue in which Clement C. Moore's classic, "The Night Before Christmas" (originally entitled "A Visit From St. Nicholas") first appeared. Penned for the amusement of the author's children, it was delivered to the *Sentinel* editor by a friend of Moore's, who felt that his marvelously convincing "eyewitness" account of the Christmas Eve visit from the "right jolly old elf" traveling in "a miniature sleigh drawn by eight tiny reindeer" deserved a wider audience. Owners of well-preserved copies of that particular issue of the *Troy Sentinel* can just about name their own price for this historic piece of Americana.

America's first good look at its own idea of St. Nick came twenty-five years later.

The original publication of Clement Moore's poem was not illustrated. An 1830 broadside edition of the poem printed in Troy, New York, did include one illustration, but it was not until 1848 that the poem was first accorded the form in which it still is sold today — the fully illustrated pamphlet edition. The Onderdonk Company of New York commissioned Theodore C. Boyd, a local engraver, to design and illustrate its new eight-page version of the Christmas classic. In the seven woodcuts done for the booklet, Boyd portrayed St. Nicholas as a short, rotund fellow with a large nose, wearing a short jacket and knee breeches. The sleigh that pulls him through the town is indeed pulled by "eight tiny reindeer —" so tiny, in fact (their antlers barely reach St. Nick's knees), that one wonders how they managed to haul their tremendous cargo.

Surviving copies of the original 1848 illustrated edition are extremely rare. Onderdonk's books were paperbound, and lacked the protection of a hard binding. Less than half a dozen copies are known to exist in collections. One that surfaced at a 1934 book dealers' auction sold for $1000. Most collectors feel that other well-preserved copies exist. One can only speculate on their present-day value! Dover Publications of New York, which issued a facsimile edition a few years ago, put it clearly: "The 1848 edition of 'A Visit From St. Nicholas' is one of the rarest items in American literature."

Closest of all the nineteenth century portrayals to our present notion of Santa Claus were those done by Thomas Nast. Nast, who also invented the donkey and elephant symbols for the Democratic and Republican parties, is best known for his political cartoons in *Harper's Weekly* during the 1860's and 1870's. (One series of Nast cartoons was instrumental in revealing the corruption in New York's Tammany Hall machine, a revelation that caused the downfall of its leader, Boss Tweed.) But Nast also bestowed on a whole generation the popularly accepted image of an American Santa Claus. *Harper's Weekly* was the forum first to present Nast's happy and elfin St. Nick.

Thomas Nast was only twenty-two when he joined *Harper's*. The nation was into the second year of the Civil War, and Nast had been hired to illustrate leading news stories of the day. His Civil War Santa shared a large part in his coverage of the war during these years. Nast's first *Harper's* Santa was introduced in the December 26, 1863 issue, in a large illustration titled "A Christmas Furlough." His 1864 drawing, "Christmas in Camp," shows Santa wearing a suit decorated for the occasion with the "Stars & Stripes," arriving by reindeer-drawn sleigh at a battle-weary Union camp hung with banners proclaiming "Welcome Santa Claus."

One of the most desirable of the early Nast Santas, from a collecting standpoint, is the large two-page illustration published in the December 29, 1866 issue of *Harper's*. Titled "Santa Claus and His Works," this drawing would in time become the basis for countless Christmas drawings by other artists. Included were scenes of a fur-clad Santa about two feet tall going about his chores at his North Pole workshop: looking through his book of good boys and girls, stitching doll clothes, sawing a rocking horse, plotting out his course with a telescope and whisking off through the night air. This composite provided the country with its first intimate look into Santa's workshop; the detail was so convincing that one would almost think that *Harper's Weekly* had sent Thomas Nast directly to the North Pole.

The *Harper's* Santas drawn by Nast are still among the most

Below left: *Tiny (3½ by 2 inches) copy of "A Visit from St. Nicholas" in color, published circa 1870 by L. Prang & Co. of Boston.* Below right: *In France, St. Nicholas rode a horse. He carries switching rods for bad children.*

And then in a twinkling I heard on the roof,
The prancing and pawing of each little hoof.
As I drew in my head, and was turning around,
Down the chimney St. Nicholas came with a bound.
He was dressed all in fur from his head to his foot,

d his clothes were all tarnished with ashes and soot;
bundle of toys he had flung on his back,
d he looked like a pedler just opening his pack.
eyes how they twinkled! his dimples how merry!
cheeks were like roses, his nose like a cherry;
droll little mouth was drawn up like a bow,

Above, left and right: *Miniature bone-china Santas an inch and a quarter high; rare pair of cast-iron Santas.* Below: *Antique Christmas cards — note silk fringes and tassels.*

widely reproduced of all Santa likenesses. Consequently, original issues of *Harper's* containing Nast's drawings are popular with collectors. Victorians were in the habit of framing the large double-page prints and hanging them on parlor walls and in children's rooms. Such preserved copies of "Santa Claus And His Works," and the other holiday Nast drawings, turn up in antique shops among the usual selection of Madonna prints and veterinarian degrees, for $35 to $50. Dealers' prices are much higher. The condition of the paper is the major factor in determining the price of a print. The large pages of *Harper's* were printed on newspaper stock, which, unless framed, in time became extremely fragile.

In 1876 Clement Moore's poem appeared under a now more familiar title, "The Night Before Christmas," in an edition published by the Dutton Company of New York. Soon other publishers picked up the new title. In 1886, McLoughlin of New York issued one of the first full-color editions of "The Night Before Christmas" as part of a "Christmas Eve Series." Here Santa has grown quite a bit — up to about four feet, and what's more, acquired a wife! This was the first appearance of Mrs. Claus.

Early greeting cards are actively collected by Christmas buffs. The color card process was introduced by Bostonian Louis Prang, who produced the Christmas (and New Year) penny postcards of the era. Prang's company had a yearly card output of almost five million, rivalling England's famous "Tuck" cards by Raphael Tuck & Sons. The Boston card manufacturer continued to lead in card production until the advent of the folded Christmas cards we know today.

Although Christmas postcards often ignored the traditional trappings and *dramatis personae* of the season, Santa gradually gained popularity as a subject. It was a postcard artist who first elevated Santa to full adult height, and postcard artists who discarded the old fur garb in favor of more colorful apparel. Santa postcards picturing him wearing blue, green and other unusually colored coats are of especial interest to collectors dating as they do from before the time that all agreed that Santa wears a red coat. One novelty card from the twenties showed Santa sporting a cosmopolitan flair — wearing colored goggles, a jaunty touring cap, and driving an open roadster — reindeer, if any, presumably concealed under the hood. Cards like this, showing Santa in unusual situations or costumes, may be worth up to $10, while other less distinctive cards may be very inexpensive. Often a whole collection may change hands for $5 to $10. Folded greeting cards with envelopes as sold today are not collectable, although in time collections of such cards may well acquire value.

Every famous magazine artist of the 1920's-1940's had at least one try at capturing Santa on canvas for the covers of a family magazine. In his first year with *The Saturday Evening Post,* illustrator Norman Rockwell chose to use St. Nick on his first Christmas cover, painted for the December 9, 1916 issue, his sixth cover for the *Post.* The Norman Rockwell Santa was to visit *Post* covers frequently — in 1920, 1922, 1924, 1926 and for years to

St. Nicholas in the Twentieth Century as painted by Norman Rockwell (left) and Haddon Sundbloom (right). Sundbloom always used himself as the model for his Santa Claus paintings.

follow. Today, these Christmas issues will bring $18-$20 or more each from collectors.

Nostalgia collectors are rediscovering the famous soft drink Santas of Haddon Sundblom. The Santas which Sundblom painted in Coca-Cola advertisements showed up regularly each December from 1931 to 1968 on the back covers of most leading magazines. Many Americans grew up with the Sundblom Santa and can readily recall their first glimpse of him, whether on a cardboard standup at a hometown general store or beaming his happy smile from a huge billboard atop a downtown city building. Since most of Sundblom's work has been commercial in nature, it is not signed. His first commercial contract came back in the twenties, when he did a few canvases for the Quaker Oats Company. The company's familiar Quaker who appears on nearly all their products was painted by Sundblom, as was the portrait of Mrs. Anna Robinson, better known as "Aunt Jemima." She was a very real

person, who died in 1951, but her likeness lives on in super-markets across the country.

Of the many commercial ventures in Sundblom's long career, his thirty-seven Santa "portraits" for Coca-Cola proved to be the American public's favorite. Sundblom's Santas abound with spirit and life, in radiant colors, and show the good fellow in situations to which we all can relate: raiding the icebox when no one is looking, pausing to have a little fun with the toys, or enjoying the chance to relax after some particularly long hours. Always painting from live models, Sundblom never had to venture far for his Santa pictures. Possessing a striking resemblance to jolly old St. Nick minus the beard, the artist painted his own face behind that white fluff in the Coke ads all those years!

Coca-Cola Santa magazine ads by Sundblom bring $5-$10 each if published in the 1930's-1940's; more current ads are worth less — $2-$3.

Christmas collectors are fortunate in being immersed the year round in the magical spirit of Christmas that, like Santa Claus, visits most of us only once a year. □ □

A replica of New England's first recorded Christmas tree, that of Dr. Charles Follen, decorated with candles, beads, birds, and angels. Gilded eggshell halves hold tissue paper; cornucopias are filled with candy.

Halloweeniana

The goblins'll get you if you don't watch out!

HALLOWEEN is when we celebrate things that go bump in the night, the day preceding All Saints' Day, the time set aside by the Roman Catholic Church to honor all the saints not provided with a special day of their own in the ecclesiastical calendar. All Saints' Day dates back to 609 A.D., when Pope Boniface IV dedicated the Pantheon to the Virgin Mary and all martyrs. By 900 A.D., the date was set as November 1. Medieval England termed All Saints' Day All Hallows (All Holies), and the day before became Hallows' eve, or Halloween. Since November 1 belonged to the saints, logically enough October 31 was set aside for the opposite sort of beings — witches, goblins, imps, devils, and the like.

A big event of small-town American life for years was the annual Halloween masquerade party, celebrated with apple-bobbing, pumpkin pie, fortune telling, cider and pin-the-tail-on-the-donkey, with colorful costumes sported by all. Families would pore over magazines and catalogues weeks in advance looking for just the right gaudery. "A witch's costume always offers opportunities for an amazing and truly effective disguise," the October 1913 issue of *The Delineator* told readers. The 1900 Butterick Patterns catalogue demonstrated how a family could be transformed by bizarre costumes into Japanese lanterns, clowns, Etruscan vases, a deck of cards, monarch butterflies and frogs. Halloween was a time to forget dull care, a time to celebrate, a time to dress up and pretend to be someone (or something) else.

The country is currently witnessing renewed interest in Halloween. "Halloween is becoming a family holiday again," a Boston costume shop owner told me. "The Halloween costume party is seeing a definite revival." Not only does this seem a fair assessment, with people flocking to costume shops in record numbers each year, but Halloween and all its paraphernalia has aroused the interest of collectors. Halloween Americana has arrived; "Halloweeniana" includes any artifact of the nineteenth or early twentieth centuries dealing with the celebration of Halloween. This includes old Halloween books, articles, songs, poems, cards, cardboard black cats and skeletons, papier-mâché masks and pumpkins, and, of course, wonderful old costumes.

Printed Halloweeniana, especially vintage Halloween books, is good value. Orne's *Halloween: Its Origin and How to Celebrate It With Appropriate Games and Ceremonies,* published in 1898 by Dick & Fitzgerald of New York (a "must" for all party planners in its day) is now worth $35. Kelley's *The Book Of Halloween,* first published by Lothrop, Lee & Shepard of Boston in 1919, is priced around $20. Even children's books are worthwhile. One artistic volume, *Tomson's Halloween,* (a 1929 picture-story of a witch's cat) illustrated by silhouettist Mary Baker, is bringing up to $15.

Song sheet from the October, 1903 issue of The Household Ledger *provides a suitable backdrop for the inset bevy of spooks. The tall Devil wears an antique (circa 1875) costume of maroon velvet studded with rhinestones. The costume includes suit (with tail), shoes, belt, cape, ascot, and hat (with ears).*

All Hallows Eve has inspired a multitude of poetic lines which were widely circulated on penny postcards during the now collectable period. Some of these poems are beautiful, others are frankly atrocious. But for every bad verse, there are also classics, like Oliver Wendell Holmes' "Broomstick Train: Or Return of the Witches;"

Look out! Look out, boys! Clear the track!
The witches are here! They've all come back!
On their well-trained broomsticks mounted high
Seen like shadows against the sky;
Crossing the tracks of owls and bats,
Hugging before them their coal-black cats. *

The family magazines of the era devoted a great deal of space yearly to Halloween. Consequently, the October issues of early twentieth century magazines provide collectors with a choice selection of Halloweeniana. In the October 1903 copy of *The Household-Ledger,* the Otto Auerbach song "A Halloween Frolic" was unveiled. It is somewhat difficult to picture adults standing around a parlor piano singing "A little witch in steeple hat once tried a merry spell/To make the hares come pit-a-pat from dingle and from dell" — but no doubt many did. The *Woman's Home Companion,* meanwhile, was providing homemakers with recipes for such less-than-tempting Halloween appetizers as Black-Cat Jelly, Wart Cake, Bat's Wings, Demon's Draught, Sorcerer's

* As quoted in: *Halloween, Its Origin, Spirit, Celebration and Significance.* Ed. Robert Haven Schauffler. *Our American Heritage* series. Dodd Mead & Co., New York, 1933, page 233.

Surprise and (honestly) Sand Witches. Demon's Draught, by the way, was made of spinach juice, and Sorcerer's Surprise was a similar concoction with hot peppers!

In America, Halloween isn't right somehow without black cats, dancing skeletons and pumpkin decorations. Pressed black-dyed cardboard (still used in Halloween products today) was first used in macabre decorations during the late nineteenth century. Hunching cats and movable jointed skeletons became early favorites. A leading manufacturer for years is the Dennison Company of Framingham, Massachusetts. Formed in 1844 to produce jewelry boxes, the company entered the Halloween products field in the early 1900's. During the teens, Dennison marketed crepe paper and pressed cardboard novelties for Halloween decorations; so many, in fact, that for eight years (1912-1920) the company published its own annual Halloween publication, *Dennison's Bogie Book*. The *Bogie Book* was filled with decorating ideas, games, stories, recipes and all kinds of Halloween magic. "Halloween is the night when a magic spell enthralls the earth," the 1912 *Bogie Book* said. "Witches rule. All things creeping have no fear. Superstition proves true, witchery asserts itself and the future may be read in a thousand ways." The 1917 issue showed how an entire ballroom could be decorated for Halloween with fifty rolls of crepe paper, six dozen festoons, and seemingly endless streamers, garlands and other decorations for merely $15. Copies of the *Bogie Book* are eagerly sought by Halloween buffs. Because Dennison's popular

The Dennison company published a number of magazines featuring novel ideas for parties, costumes, and decorations. Left to right: *Pages from the 1930 "Halloween Number" of* Parties; *cover of the earlier* Bogie Book *(1912).* Above: *Decoration popular in the '20's and '30's.*

Below: *Halloween postcard, circa 1905.* Right: *Greeting card of the same era by Raphael Tuck & Sons of London.*

cardboard cats, skeletons and other products sold by the crateloads in the 1920's, many are still to be found. As a result, only the most extravagant have collecting value today. Nevertheless, all make interesting additions to a collection, and will doubtless increase in value as their numbers inevitably decline.

Another leading manufacturer of Halloween paper products is the Beistle Company of Shippensburg, Pennsylvania, which has been busily turning out multitudes of paper pumpkins, owls, ghosts and scarecrows since the beginning of the century. Founder Martin L. Beistle's company saw the light of day in the basement workshop of his Pittsburgh home in 1900. Here Beistle would hand cut, hand fold and hand color scores of holiday products each day. In 1904, Beistle set up shop in the second story of the wagon shop in Oakville, Pennsylvania. The business grew and eventually moved to Shippensburg in 1907, where a large plant was constructed. Here company workers assembled marvelous paper creations and developed such innovations as the delicate honeycomb art-tissue products. A very popular decoration, Beistle art-tissue pumpkins were hung by the hundreds from ballroom ceilings for the fabulous Halloween costume balls which graced the era.

Many companies made extensive use of papier-mâché in those pre-rubber and pre-plastic days. Fifty-year-old papier mâché Jack-o'-lanterns are now being tagged at between $10 and $15 each. Halloween papier-mâché masks are as valuable as they are fragile. Having a tendency to chip or flake, these early masks are difficult to find in collectable condition. Those that can be found range from the cherubic to the grotesque. Papier-mâché masks of witches, devils and other horribles may be priced at from $35 to $50 if they are in top shape.

Unquestionably the most bewitching collectibles in the field are complete Halloween masquerade costumes, particularly those dating from the 1870's-1920's. Clothing archivists and private collectors are always on the lookout for these material treasures; tucked away somewhere in attics, these beautiful costumes, when discovered, can be worth hundreds of dollars.

Halloween costumes were first introduced to America by Irish immigrants during the 1840's, and by the 1870's masquerade parties were in full fling on these shores. The first American costumes were handmade from patterns. A leading early distributor of Halloween costume patterns was Ebenezer Butterick of Sterling, Massachusetts. Butterick (whose company today remains a leader in the pattern field and is based in New York) entered the business in 1863. Among his first masquerade patterns was "The

Bat," a full-length costume featuring a three-foot wing span of black sateen. Come what might — goblin gowns, devil's duds or witch's wear — "The Bat" remained the best-seller for years. Early costume patterns by Butterick and contemporaries are sought by collectors as well as the actual costumes made from them. Halloween patterns of the 1920's are worth from $5 to $10, while paper patterns dating from the 1870's to 1890's can bring upwards of $20 each. (The advent of "ready-made" costumes early in the 1900's put a damper on the pattern trade.)

America's earliest costume rental shops made all their own costumes. Foremost for years was the Hayden Costume Company in Boston. Located on Washington Street, Hayden was established in 1868 and stayed in business for over seventy-five years. Their 1900 catalogue offered eighty-four different costumes from which to choose. On occasion, Hayden would sell costumes to the public.

A 1914 Halloween print.

An elaborate and aristocratic children's Christmas party was described in the October 1853 issue of Godey's Lady's Book, *under the title:* GOSSIP FROM OUR PARIS CORRESPONDENT.

A juvenile fancy ball given last week in Paris by the Duchess de Choisieul, excited a high degree of interest. We subjoin descriptions of the most remarkable costumes worn by the youthful guests on the occasion: —

The young Prince de Polignac, who appeared in the character of Bacchus, wore a tiger-skin loosely thrown over a tunic of white gauze, to which were attached bunches of grapes and vine-leaves. His sandals were of bright red hue.

The little Duchess of Albufera was attired in a Polish dress; with a vest and caraco of white *reps* she wore a jupe of blue reps; the vest was trimmed with a torsade and *grelots* of gold. The caraco fitting close to the figure at the back, was ornamented with a torsade and *grelots* of gold. A Polish cap, edged with a band of ermine, and ornamented with a white *aigrette,* completed the beautiful and becoming costume.

The youthful Duke of Albufera wore a Biscayan costume. The trousers and waistcoat were of black velvet, the latter fastened by chased gold buttons. The jacket was composed of light-blue velvet, ornamented with gold buttons, tassels, and other ornaments in cerise and blue velvet. A silk scarf in a variety of brilliant shades of color, encircled the waist of the young mountaineer. His sombrero, or broad-brimmed hat, was made of red chenille, embroidered in crochet. The hat was encircled with a band of gold braid.

Cupid was personified by one of the very youngest of the guests. This little boy, a fine specimen of infantine beauty, was attired in a tunic of blue gauze, figured with silver stars. He was armed with a bow covered with light-blue velvet — the string, being formed of a narrow band of silver braid, and the quiver was filled with silver arrows.

The young Baron de Rothschild was dressed in a French military costume, that of the *Gardes Francais.*

The Marquis de Las Marismas, as a Shepherdess of the reign of Louis Quinze, and the little Comtesse de Pierres, as a Shepherdess in the Watteau style of dress.

Some of the most beautiful of their time, these costumes are the dream of every modern-day collector. The two-piece Hayden elephant suit (a monstrous affair of gray cloth and papier-mâché tusks) is worth up to $400. Costumes made by other early costumers, such as Krause in Cleveland (established in 1867) and Fierberg's in Hartford, Connecticut, (established in 1900), are also "such stuff as dreams are made on." Fierberg's earliest costumes were made in Romania; many were sold to royalty for European costume balls.

Of the myriad masquerade costumes produced during the early years, nearly all have some degree of collectability today. Generally speaking, adult-sized costumes of witches, bats, black cats, skeletons, devils and elaborate ghosts are of the greatest interest to Halloween collectors. "A good devil's suit from the 1890's can easily bring $200 to $300 from a collector," one Halloween buff told me. Early animal, frog, butterfly and novelty costumes are also actively sought. Clown, foreign-dress and period costumes, although collectable, are seldom worth more than $50 unless they date before 1900. It takes a lot of perseverance to find early costumes. But as one collector said to me after an exhaustive search which turned up an original 1886 witch's costume complete with peaked hat and black cape (estimated worth: $250), "Believe me, they're worth it!"

Where did he look? Everywhere that came to mind. He perused the advertisements in collectibles and antiques news sheets and magazines regularly, and in turn advertised in their "wanted" columns. He asked everyone he knew, visited costume museums and archives. Actually, the costume turned up among the belongings of an elderly couple who, having decided to move south, held a yard sale to dispose of everything that had accumulated in their house and attic over the past fifty years!

Children's costumes are also sought, but on a lesser scale. The notion of "Trick or Treat" which started in the 1920's and gained popularity increasingly through the sixties gave rise to mass-produced children's costumes — many thousands cheaply made and sold. Montgomery Ward began selling sets of six masks (made of hard gauze) for 29¢ and full costumes for under a dollar. As a result children's costumes are far more common than their adult-size counterparts, though a few of the more innovative do have collectable value. One company offered a "glow-in-the-dark ghost sheet" for a time during the 1920's. At night these costumes shone brilliantly thanks to a phosphorus additive. A great breakthrough, it was hailed, until parents found that tykes caught in the rain while wearing the "ghost sheet" continued to glow for days after — without the costume! It disappeared from the market shortly thereafter.

It may be merely a coincidence that the sudden fascination with early American Halloween artifacts comes just as costume shops are reporting unprecedented interest in Halloween costumes. In any case, clearly Halloween is still alive and well and still giving us the opportunity to plunge into fantasy for that one night of the year. □ □

Valentines Galore

Hearts, flowers, and the Civil War

PERHAPS the first holiday collectibles to be recognized as such were antique valentines. People have been collecting them for years, as these missives of Cupid date back to the first half of the 1800's. For many, early valentines mean the delicately-cut paper creations bearing sentimental verses; one such printed in the 1880's asks tenderly — *Wilt thou be mine, Dear love, reply. Sweetly consent, or else deny; Whisper softly, none shall know. Wilt thou be mine, yes or no?* But then as now, there was a second type of valentine — comic valentine or "February Fools" cards. First popular during the mid-nineteenth century, these conveyed a totally different type of message that often held a sting. One comic valentine read, *If the truth must be told, you cut it all too fine; You're a smart-looking blade, but no favorite of mine.* Ouch!

The holiday first began to gain recognition in this country during the early nineteenth century. In 1853, *Gleason's Pictorial* tried to decide how it all got started: "St. Valentine's Day is being more and more generally observed in this country," *Gleason's* told its readers. "And though thousands upon thousands partake in the usual sports and habits of the occasion, few pause to consider the origin of the institution."

Actually, the February 14th holiday goes back to the Roman festival of Lupercalia, held every year in ancient Rome in mid-February to celebrate the rites of spring and ensure renewed fertility. When Christianity became the official religion of the Roman Empire by edict of the Emperor Constantine, popular pagan festivals were retained, but renamed and reframed to fit the new religion. St. Valentine, stoned to death on February 14, 270 A.D., lent his name to the Christianized version of Lupercalia. With the passage of time — from the Middle Ages on — sentiment rather than sexuality gradually became the focus of the day. As the centuries passed, the martyred saint turned into the kindly patron of shy lovers who wish to express their true feelings for another, with the option of remaining incognito. *Within the mirror you will see, all that is beautiful to me,* promises a valentine of 1890. (Cupid, of course, was a Roman god!)

Collectors recognize a number of different categories of American valentines, each of which has its own enthusiasts. First are the cards issued during the initial period of lithographed valentines, those printed during the years 1840-1860. Comic valentines, very popular in the fifties and sixties, are collected both for their satire and for their part in the development of comic art in this country. Civil War valentines are very rare and today are the highest-priced of all. And, of course, there is a good deal of interest in those beautiful lacy creations belonging to the late Victorian period.

Printed valentines first burst on the American scene during the 1840's (prior to that time, valentines were all handmade). While a few of the first commercially marketed valentines were engraved or made from woodcut blocks, most were lithographed and hand-colored.

America's first major producer of valentines was Thomas W. Strong of New York. His wholesale and retail publishing and engraving business got underway in 1842 with valentines being a specialty. "Strong's Grand Valentine Depot," as his shop on Nassau Street was called, covered the entire gamut of valentines, as promised in an 1848 advertisement: "Valentines! Valentines! All varieties of Valentines, imported and domestic, sentimental, humorous, witty, comic, serious, locals, and nationals, got up in the most superb style on lace paper and gold, without regard to expense." You could buy a Strong card for anywhere from 6¢ to $10, depending on how lavish an impression you wanted to make. The coloring was all done by hand. Strong cards can be identified by the words: "Strong, N.Y.;" "T. W. Strong, 98 Nassau St., N.Y.;" or simply "98 Nassau St." Early Strong valentines, whether comic or romantic, cost today between $15 and $30. Two other pioneer producers of American valentines who were flourishing as early as the 1840's were Turner & Fisher of Philadelphia, and Elton & Company of New York.

Comic valentines arrived on these shores from England,

Top: *For home-assembled valentines, you'd use a box of small chromolithographed cut-outs, paper lace, card blanks or bases, paste, and stiff paper strips to fold for hinges (like the one showing to the right of the girl pictured in the valentine left).* Below left: *Civil War valentine.* Center and right: *Comic valentines with a bite.*

Above: Silver lace paper, three tiers of sentiment on accordion-pleated hinges, plenty of colorful cut-outs (the girl is hinged to stand out from her background) make this a Victorian whimsy indeed. Left: This folded card opens to a printed message. Envelope flaps on cover fold out (this is a large cut-out). Circa 1900.

where "penny dreadfuls," as Britons called them, made up the bulk of the cards sold in the British Isles during the holiday. While a few of these cards poked mild fun, many were downright mean, with cards bearing titles like "To a Bad Dancer" or "To a Stingy Fellow" among the selection. Cards with venomous verses first appeared in America about 1841. Their darts were aimed at one and all — the poor and lowly, rich and pompous, young and old. Fashionably dressed ladies and gentlemen were popular subjects with valentine cartoonists, as were many of the fads of the day.

McLoughlin Brothers of New York specialized in comic valentines. First issued in 1848, McLoughlin cards were distinguished by bold colors, with vivid reds and greens obtained by overlapping color printing, in which each card was run through the

Commercial valentines. The three-tiered card above left is 9 inches high and stands on its own base. Right, above: *Embossed postcard valentine.* Below: *Flowers carried by bride and groom and those on bride's skirt are made of tiny glass beads.*

press two or three times. The company prospered for years, publishing a long line of paper goods, including children's books. In the early 1940's, McLoughlin Brothers moved to Springfield, Massachusetts, where its priceless archives were stored in a warehouse basement. The collection, which included early catalogues and sample books containing thousands of the valentines issued during the nineteenth century, was destroyed by a flood a short time later. Comic valentines published by McLoughlin and others have a market all their own and are particularly favored by collectors of early American comic art.

Sentimentality in the printed form reached a zenith during the Civil War. Husbands taken from their wives and families, sweethearts separated — the war made these common occurrences on both sides of the Mason-Dixon Line. Quick to pick up the theme, valentine producers issued scores of cards picturing bittersweet farewells or soldiers gathered around the campfire writing to dear ones back home. Fueled by the loneliness of war, valentine sales soared. The American Valentine Company of New York offered special packets of cards for soldiers; ladies could select the "Soldier Valentine Packet," the "American Valentine Packet," or the "Torch of Love Packet." Typical of the scenes pictured on these cards was one showing a battalion of Cupids

". . . there is pansies, that's for thoughts."

dressed in Union Blue and marching in formation, shouldering their love arrows like rifles.

Another producer, M. T. Cozans of New York, ran an ad in the February 8, 1862 issue of *Harper's Weekly* (two days after Grant's Northern troops captured Fort Henry), announcing over a thousand different valentines available for purchase by soldiers at prices ranging from 3¢ to 10¢ apiece. One valentine nowadays considered very desirable is a tent made from the Stars and Stripes, which opens to reveal a Union soldier seizing a tranquil moment to write a letter home. The image of his loved one is faintly visible over his shoulder.

Civil War era valentines have been in demand for years, not only among valentine collectors, but by Civil War buffs as well. Meanwhile, stamp collectors vie for the envelopes they came in, bearing the postmarks of the various theaters of the war. With all these collectors striving for what is essentially a small number of surviving cards, the search has been intense and the prices very high. Many single cards have exceeded the $75-$100 range, with the Confederate cards, issued in lesser numbers, commanding prices twice those of their Union counterparts.

When one thinks of valentines of the nineteenth century, what usually comes to mind are marvelously delicate lace-edged creations, extravagantly embellished with hearts, cupids and flowers. These cards had their origin in this country in a Worcester, Massachusetts, home.

Esther Howland is credited with having been the "Mother of the American Valentine." Authorities differ as to whether she or Strong was the first to produce valentines commercially here, but her company certainly did become the leader in its field. As the story goes, Miss Howland, the daughter of a Worcester stationer, had received a lithographed card from England shortly after her graduation from college. Very impressed by it, she was inspired to create a few cards of her own, decorated with small lithographed figures and flowers. Her brother, who worked as a salesman for their father, took these sample cards with him on the road in 1847. When he returned, he had orders for five thousand valentines. Miss Howland immediately set to work to fill the demand, turning her home into a workshop and hiring local girls to help assemble cards. Embossed and perforated lace paper blanks were ordered from England, the only country producing them at the time, and the small colored figures and other needed trimmings were acquired from one George Snyder, a New York lithographer. An assembly line system was set up in the Howland home, with each girl applying a different embellishment to the cards as they passed along. As demands increased, Miss Howland introduced new materials to her cards, including silk and satin. From these modest beginnings was to come a $100,000-a-year enterprise, outselling all competitors.

Howland originals can be identified by the small "H" which was stamped in red on either the upper or lower corner of each card issued. Often the "H" is accompanied by numerals, believed to refer to the card's size (the cards were not dated). In the early

1870's, Miss Howland's prosperous company took the name, New England Valentine Company; cards made from that time on bore the initials "N.E.V.Co." Miss Howland continued to lead the field in sentimental valentines until 1880, when the illness of her parents prompted her to sell out to the George C. Whitney Company, a rival Worcester firm. Esther Howland dropped out of the public eye shortly thereafter. Ironically, this woman, who had made a fortune by creating tokens of love for others, died a spinster at the age of seventy-five in Quincy, Massachusetts, in the year 1904.

The cards she left behind are today considered among the most beautiful paper creations of the nineteenth century. Prices today for Howland cards depend on their condition (being delicately made, they are often found with pieces of decoration or lace missing), and on their complexity. Cards that stood up or folded over always attract a collector's eye. Prices seen for Howland cards in recent years range from a few dollars each for some of the more common cards of the 1870's, to $15 and $20 for those dating from the 1840's and 1850's.

The turn of the century saw advancements in production technology which made valentine manufacture faster and cheaper and less expensive. Cards could now be printed by machines, colored by machines, cut by machines and assembled by machines. The production of lace-trimmed valentines declined sharply.

Most collectors date the end of the original period of the American valentine at 1917 when, as a result of World War I, production of non-essential materials was at a low ebb. In time, however, more contemporary examples of Cupid's missives will enter the realm of collectibles. Already the valentines of the 1920's, with their images of rosy-cheeked children, have been welcomed into some of the newer collections. As the original valentines of the 1800's become more and more difficult to acquire with each passing year, their twentieth century successors will continue to grow in collectable value.

Where to look for valentines? Boxes of old letters and papers and old scrapbooks are likely places — you can turn these up at estate auctions or in your neighbor's attic (or your own!). Other collectors and ads in the antiques and collectibles journals are also good sources. Just keep in mind that loose cards are generally more valuable than those pasted down in scrapbooks. But if you do turn up a lode of valentines preserved in a scrapbook, keep them there — don't try to remove them but treat the entire scrapbook as a collectable unit.

Valentines represent the most intimate of all collectibles, being souvenirs of the heart. One of the most interesting I have ever seen was a simple white card, embossed with miniature hearts. The card, inscribed in a feminine hand "February 14, 1854," held no message — just a single lock of hair. Whether it was sent as a token of friendship, or as an acceptance of a proposal of marriage, one can only guess. The sender of the card and the young suitor who received it are both long gone. Only the valentine and its precious contents endure. □ □

Section 4

Riding the Rails
and
Hitting the Road

Railroadiana

RAILROAD buffs will stop at nothing in their infatuation for the lore of the rails. "We eat on dining car china, light our homes with rail lanterns, read early timetables, wear old conductor's uniforms and cover our walls with steam locomotive posters. Our garages look like train wrecks!" Families of railroadiana collectors put it more simply — "It's sort of like living in Grand Central Station."

Enter the home of a bona fide buff, and you get the uncanny feeling that the 6:05 southbound will be passing through the living room at any minute. Collectors of railroad memorabilia are united by the Railroadiana Collectors Association (405 Byron Avenue, Mobile, AL 36609), incorporated in 1971. Membership numbers over five hundred and is growing. Secretary-Treasurer Dan Moss informed me, "We have never had a national convention, but do hold many regional meetings." The group publishes an attractive and profusely illustrated quarterly, *The Railroadiana Express*. Recent issues have featured articles about travel — a tour of the Union Pacific Historical Museum in Omaha, for example; collecting — collecting railroad menus; as well as pertinent book reviews, advertisements and even railroad-inspired poetry. Railroadiana collectors rely on advertisements to a high degree — and are possibly more dependent on them for communication and information than are collectors in other fields, although swop sessions, shows and conventions also provide good hunting grounds.

Stop, Look, Listen — and Collect!

According to the Railroadiana Collectors Association, there are three types of railroad collectors: those who collect all railroad-related memorabilia; those who specialize in railroad hardware; and those primarily concerned with railroad paper. Railroadiana comprises an almost infinite number of items, as anything which generates the magic of early steam can be considered a potential collectible — all the way from luxurious private cars to tiny railroad-union pins. There are certain artifacts, however, that are consistently in demand.

One example is timetables, sought by collectors because they record the daily schedules of long-vanished railroads. A yellowed timetable can tell you exactly when the Grand Trunk Railroad came barrelling through your home town in 1914. Pre-1880 timetables consisted merely of the train's hourly connections printed on a plain single card. But with advances in color lithography in the late nineteenth century, timetables became beautiful folders which not only told you arrival and departure times, but also all about the "zenith of luxury" offered by the new Pullman cars and the history of the countryside you'd be traveling through, generously illustrated with maps and pictures. Timetables from 1880-1890 are worth $20 or more, depending on the complexity and style of the graphic art. Even more recent timetables are marketable. A 1949 Boston & Maine timetable, for example, is worth $5.00.

Clockwise from far left below: *Bangor & Aroostook R.R. "whistle post," indicator of a highway crossing; Boston and Maine container to hold drinking water and glasses for thirsty train crews (1890's); Northern R.R. whale-oil hand lantern (1840's), ball signal lantern and kerosene hand lantern (both 1900's); sand-containing fire bucket (1885); 1920's Baltimore & Ohio dinnerware — the platter pictures Indian Gap, the plate, Harper's Ferry; "Keystone State" Pennsylvania R.R. locomotive number plate.*

BOSTON AND MAINE R. R.

LIST OF FREIGHT AND PASSENGER REPRESENTATIVES

Buffalo, N. Y. — 416 Ellicott Sq. Bldg. (Phone Seneca 0476)
  GROVER C. ALDRICH, General Agent.

Caribou, Me. — O. L. PERKINS, Traffic Representative.

Chicago, Ill. — Utilities Bldg., 327 So. LaSalle St. (Phone Harrison 0672)
  H. B. GARVEY, General Western Agent.
  H. F. MOCKLAR, Commercial Agent.
  I. R. LITH, Traffic Representative
  F. N. MAYER, Traffic Representative.
  G. E. KANE, Passenger Representative.

Cleveland, Ohio. — 509 Park Building. (Phone Main 5757)
  T. D. ELLIOTT, General Agent.

Concord, N. H. — (Phone Concord 29-J).
  I. N. DOE, Division Freight Agent.
  R. W. ADAMS, Traveling Freight Agent.

Detroit, Mich. — 5-135 General Motors Building. (Phone Northway 5520)
  J. J. WRIGHT, General Agent.
  B. A. BUSHELL, Traffic Representative.
  W. A. KNIPE, Traffic Representative.

Kansas City, Mo. — 515 Railway Exchange Building. (Phone Victor 1579)
  R. C. CHAMBON, General Agent.

Memphis, Tenn. — 422-423 Cotton Exchange Building. (Phone 8-6124)
  H. H. SCHUTT, General Agent.

New York City — 910 Woolworth Bldg. (Phone Whitehall 3730-3731)
  W. H. LODGE, General Agent.
  W. J. SHANLEY, Traffic Representative.

Philadelphia, Pa. — 425 Widener Building. (Phone Rittenhouse 4xxx)
  C. H. KELEHER, General Agent.

Pittsburgh, Pa. — 961 Union Trust Bldg. (Phone Atlantic 3596.
  A. F. LANE, General Agent.
  R. O. BEEBE, Traffic Representative.

Portland, Me. — 602 Congress St. (Phone Forest 113 114 115).
  E. W. ABBOTT, District Manager 6
  O. F. PATTRICK, Traffic Representative.
  H. A. BUCKLIN, Traffic Representative.
  J. P. SMITH, Traveling Passenger Agent.

St. Louis, Mo. — 1980 Railway Exchange Building. (Phone Main 3469)
  H. B. CHURCH, General Agent.

San Francisco, Cal. — 923 Monadnock Building. (Phone Kearny 1757)
  TRACY CUMMINGS, Pacific Coast Agent.

Seattle, Wash. — 567 White-Henry-Stuart Building. (Phone Main 7180)
  H. L. ANDERSON, Traffic Representative.

Springfield, Mass. — 1694 Main St. (Phone River 1987).
  W. H. SHEPHERD, District Passenger Agent.
  D. W. WATERS, Division Freight Agent.
  W. A. CHEYNE, Traveling Freight Agent.

Troy, N. Y. — Union Station.
  J. C. OTIS, Division Freight Agent.
  C. J. JONES, Traveling Freight Agent.

Worcester, Mass — Lincoln Square. (Phone Park 3215)
  J. N. GALL, District Manager §
  J. R. POWERS, Division Freight Agent.

Woodsville, N. H. — (Phone Woodsville 2)
  M. L. FULLER, Traveling Freight Agent.

§ Also in charge of local operating matters.

RAILROAD FARES VIA BOSTON

FROM	To Erie, Penn.	To Clevel'nd, Ohio	To Toledo, Ohio	To Elkhart, Ind.	To Chic'go Ill.
Auburn, Me.	$26 14	$29 56	$33 42	$38 21	$41 81
Augusta, Me.	27 08	30 50	34 36	39 15	42 75
Bangor, Me.	29 76	33 18	37 04	41 83	45 43
Bath, Me.	26 20	29 62	33 48	38 27	41 87
Beverly, Mass	21 62	25 04	28 90	33 69	37 29
Concord, N. H.	23 60	27 02	30 88	35 67	39 27
Dover, N. H.	23 39	26 81	30 67	35 46	39 06
Gardner, Me.	26 85	30 27	34 13	38 92	42 52
Gloucester, Mass	22 10	25 52	29 38	34 17	37 77
Haverhill, Mass.	22 16	25 67	29 43	34 22	37 82
Lewiston, Me.	26 17	29 59	33 45	38 24	41 84
Lowell, Mass.	21 89	25 31	29 17	33 96	37 56
Lynn, Mass	21 58	24 80	28 66	33 45	37 05
Manchester, N. H.	22 98	26 40	30 26	35 05	38 65
No. Lawrence, Mass.	22 37	25 79	29 65	34 44	38 04
Newburyport, Mass.	22 31	25 73	29 59	34 38	37 98
No. Lawrence, Mass	22 41	25 83	29 20	33 99	37 59
Pittsfield, Me.	28 52	31 94	35 80	40 59	44 19
Portland, Me.	24 88	28 30	32 16	36 95	40 55
Portsmouth, N. H.	23 02	26 44	30 30	35 09	38 69
Rockland, Me.	28 51	31 93	35 20	39 99	43 59
Salem, Mass	21 55	24 97	28 83	33 62	37 22
South Lawrence, Mass.	23 69	25 31	29 17	33 96	37 56
Waterville, Me.	27 78	31 20	35 06	39 85	43 45

RAILROAD FARES VIA GARDNER

FROM	To Erie, Penn.	To Clevel'nd, Ohio	To Toledo, Ohio	To Elkhart, Ind.	To Chic'go Ill.
Worcester, Mass	$19 46	$22 88	$26 74	$31 53	$35 13

VIA GREENFIELD

FROM	To Erie, Penn.	To Clevel'nd, Ohio	To Toledo, Ohio	To Elkhart, Ind.	To Chic'go Ill.
Bellows Falls, Vt.	$19 88	$22 30	$26 16	$30 95	$34 55
Brattleboro, Vt.	18 53	21 45	25 31	30 10	33 70
East Northfield, Mass	17 65	21 07	24 93	29 72	33 32
Holyoke, Mass.	17 82	20 94	24 80	29 59	33 19
Keene, N. H.	18 51	21 93	25 79	30 58	34 18
Northampton, Mass	17 52	20 94	24 80	29 59	33 19
Springfield, Mass	17 63	21 05	24 91	29 70	33 30
White River Jct., Vt	20 30	23 72	27 58	32 37	35 97

The time shown in this folder is
EASTERN STANDARD TIME
One hour earlier than
DAYLIGHT SAVING TIME

FOR INFORMATION

WRITE OR CALL Any Boston Main Ticket Office

City Ticket Office, 6, 6, Franklin St. (Phone Liberty 1990)
Travel Bureau   North Station.
Ticket Office   (Phone Depot 3000)
Passenger Traffic Dep.
  H. F. FIELD   W. O. WRIGHT,
Passenger Traffic Manager   General Passenger Agent

Railroads sold hundreds of passenger tickets each day during the golden age of rail travel. Today these tickets are collector's items, particularly those dating from the last years of the nineteenth century. Printed on heavy pasteboard in a rainbow assortment of colors, train tickets of this period framed in groups make attractive additions to collections. Both punched and unpunched tickets are equally sought. The holes punched in a ticket tell its story, as the conductor would punch a different cut mark into the ticket at each departure, thus these cuts — stars, triangles, crescent moons, octagons, etc. — show where the ticket buyer got on the train, what towns he passed through, and where he got off. Tickets from the 1890's go for from $4 to $8 each.

Railroad lanterns are among the most desirable forms of railroadiana. Kerosene-burning lanterns first came into use during the 1860's; before that, lanterns burned whale oil. As the lanterns were used as signals, their color is significant. Lanterns with a red glass globe signified warning; a white globe denoted direction; and the blue globe meant car repairs. The globes being breakable, it is difficult to find railroad lanterns with original glass, but if you can find them, they are of course top value. All lanterns bore the initials of their railroad embossed on both the metal base and the glass globe. A globe lacking these raised initials is probably not original. Nevertheless, a room filled with glowing red, white and blue railroad lanterns is the pride of many a collector. Models manufactured by Adlake, A & M Buck, Dressel, Handlan and

Two pages from the Boston and Maine's timetable for its crack "Minute Man".

CONNECTIONS FROM CHICAGO
TO AND FROM SPOKANE, SEATTLE AND
PORTLAND.
VIA C. M. AND ST. P. RY.
(From Union Passenger Sta.)

	P.M.		STATIONS		P.M.	A.M.
*11 00		Lv CHICAGO Ill.	Ar	*8 45	*9 25
8 00		Ar SPOKANE Wash.	Lv	8.00	8.50
7 00		SEATTLE "		8.45	8 00
8 20		Ar TACOMA "	Lv	7.15	8 00
		Daily		P.M.	A.M.

VIA M. ST. P. & S. S. M. RY. (Soo Line.)
(From Grand Cen. Sta.)

		STATIONS		A.M.	A.M.
*6 35	10 15	Lv CHICAGO Ill.	Lv	*7 15	*9 15
	12 15	Ar MINNEAPOLIS Minn.		5.05	7 05
		ST. PAUL		6.15	*7 45
		BANFF Alta.		9.45	
		LAKE LOUISE		8.15	
		VANCOUVER B.C.		7.45	
	2 30	VICTORIA		1.45	
	8 30	Ar SEATTLE Wash.		*8 00	

RAILROAD AND SLEEPING CAR FARES

Boston, Mass., to	RAIL-ROAD FARES	PULLMAN FARES (INCLUDING SURCHARGE)		
		Upper Berth	Lower Berth	Drawing Room
Erie, Penn.	$20 96	$4 50	$5 63	$21 00
Cleveland, Ohio	22 59	5 10	6 38	22 50
Toledo, Ohio	28 24	6 60	8 25	30 00
Elkhart, Ind.	34 64	7 20	9 00	31 50
Chicago, Ill.	38 63	8 10	10 13	36 00
Fitchburg, Mass., to				
Erie, Penn.	19 17	4 50	5 63	21 00
Cleveland, Ohio	22 59	5 10	6 38	22 50
Toledo, Ohio	26 45	6 60	8 25	30 00
Elkhart, Ind.	31 04	7 20	9 00	31 50
Chicago, Ill.	34 84	8 10	10 13	36 00
Gardner, Mass., to				
Erie, Penn.	18 63	4 50	5 63	21 00
Cleveland, Ohio	22 05	5 10	6 38	22 50
Toledo, Ohio	25 91	6 60	8 25	30 00
Elkhart, Ind.	30 70	7 20	9 00	31 50
Chicago, Ill.	34 30	8 10	10 13	36 00
Greenfield, Mass., to				
Erie, Penn.	17 15	3 60	4 50	18 50
Cleveland, Ohio	20 57	4 50	5 63	21 00
Toledo, Ohio	24 43	6 60	7 50	27 00
Elkhart, Ind.	29 22	6 90	8 63	31 50
Chicago, Ill.	32 82	7 20	9 00	31 50
North Adams, Mass., to				
Erie, Penn.	15 82	3 60	4 50	18 50
Cleveland, Ohio	20 24	4 50	5 63	21 00
Toledo, Ohio	23 10	6 60	7 50	27 00
Elkhart, Ind.	27 89	6 90	8 63	31 50
Chicago, Ill.	31 49	7 20	9 00	31 50

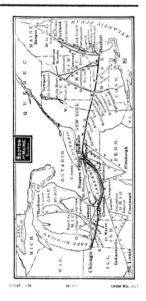

Two more pages from the 1927 summer timetable shown on page 99.

Vietz are widely sought. An Adlake 1913 lantern can bring $30 or more, while the rarer A & M Buck models from the same year, with polished brass nameplates, sell for $50.

The early railroads were very protective of their property and kept everything under lock and key. Today even these locks and keys are collectable. Most valuable are the locks and keys which guarded switches used to route trains to another track. Unlocked train switches were responsible for more than one head-on collision involving accidentally re-routed locomotives. These rust-proof brass locks and keys are very popular with a large group of railroadiana buffs. So much so that these collectors have combined with lantern enthusiasts to publish their own offset quarterly, *Key, Lock & Lantern* (Box 15, Spencerport, NY 14559). Subscribers hold a yearly convention where much railroad hardware changes hands.

A delightful part of railroadiana is dining-car collectibles — china dishes, glasses, mugs and saucers, creamers, serving trays, silverware — all the furnishings of a dining car. Every collector fantasizes stumbling upon a complete tea set from the New York, New Haven & Hartford Railroad. All railroad china is greatly desired and easily identified by the railroads' nearly universal practice of monogramming everything. It is possible for collectors, through painstaking efforts, to assemble an entire service set of one pattern. Most, however, try to collect at least one piece from every known line and leave it at that. Where a single plate may cost $35, such a collection represents a substantial investment.

Old menus are very popular collector's items and give us a wallet-tugging indication of how drastically prices have changed since the heyday of rail service. A 1910 Northern Pacific Christmas menu offered a dish of Spanish mackerel for 50¢, stuffed quail with bacon for 60¢, and sirloin steak for 80¢. An illustrated 1938 Great Northern menu recently sold for $7.50.

Some examples of prices brought by dining car collectibles are: $13 for an 1896 Boston & Albany butter knife in good condition and made by the Reed & Barton Company; $40 for a 6- by 9-inch "Vanderbilt" platter with printed ribbons and bows accentuated in gold leaf from New York Central; $18 for a New Haven "Beantown" beanpot in top condition; and $24 for a Baltimore and Ohio centennial cream pitcher.

Books, magazines, and other early railroad reading matter always find a market. There are four categories of collectable railroad books: general nonfiction, technical, adult fiction, and children's books. Most railroad-related books come under the heading of general nonfiction — books demonstrating the glamour of trains and aimed towards the general public. *The Romance of the Modern Locomotive* by Archibald Williams, published by Lippincott in 1904, now sells for $6 in very good condition. Edward Hungerford's *Locomotives on Parade* (1940), published by Crowell, goes for $14 in the original dust jacket. Many technical books are protracted tomes tedious to the average reader, but engrossing to the diehard rail buff. Leonard Jones' leather-bound *A Treatise of the Law of Railroads*, published in Boston (1879) and running over 707 pages, goes for $8 a copy. Mattias N. Forney's 609-page *Catechism of the Locomotive* (1880), published by Railroad Gazette Publishers, sells for $16 and is very hard to find. A leather-bound telegrapher's manual was recently snapped up at the asking price of $20.

Fiction stories glorifying bravery and heroics among the men of the railroad have long been popular. *The Nerve of Foley and Other Railroad Stories* by Frank H. Spearman (1900, Harper & Brothers), one of the popular railroad fiction writers of his day, held many readers on the edge of their seats. It sells for $11 today. These stories were only topped in the drama department by their juvenile counterparts, where acts of death-defying heroism happened at a rate of every dozen pages. In *Ralph in the Switch Tower* by Allen Chapman (1907, Mershon), we find the young rail hero of the book at the controls of a railroad switch tower. Suddenly Ralph discovers that a locomotive is barrelling in on a collision course with a parked train:

> The minute that Ralph's hands struck the levers, a thrill and then a chill — strong, overpowering, and deadly, paralyzed every nerve in his body.
>
> Every vestige of sensation left his frame — his hands, perfectly nerveless, seemed glued to the levers.
>
> He could not detach them, strive as he might — he could not exert a single ounce of pulling power.
>
> With a gasp Ralph saw the chaser engine dash down the rails, a hundred, eighty, seventy, fifty feet from the main

This attractive booklet distributed by the Passenger Traffic Dept. of Boston's North Station gave information on where to go and stay and special tourist fares in New England for the winter of 1922-23.

switch, so the engineer and fireman, relying on the tower service never noticed that they were headed for a tremendous crash . . .

With a sickening sense of horror Ralph strove to pull the levers.

Something was wrong! He could not move a muscle. Like one petrified he glared down at the flying locomotive, headed straight for disaster and destruction.

Few television shows can beat that for suspense!

Publications like *The Railroad Man's Magazine* are even more difficult than hard-bound books to find in good condition. The first issue of that particular magazine, October 1906, announced to all and sundry that it was "A Red-Hot Magazine for the Railroad Man or for anyone else who knows a Good Thing when he sees it." Other early rail magazines were *Locomotive Engineering, American Engineer,* and *The Railway Magazine.* They featured informative articles on subjects such as what to do if the bridge is out or how to clear the track of stray cattle.

Promotional brochures, calendars, and decks of playing cards (bearing the names of the various lines) are also collectable railroad paper. A 39-page brochure, "The First Ninety Years — 1850-1940 — an Historical Sketch of the Burlington Railroad" (1940), is valued at $8.50. A calendar issued by the Great Rock Island Route in 1892 commemorating the Chicago World's Fair sells now for $12. Decks of cards ("Railroad Bibles") were sold inexpensively by the railroads to help passengers pass the time on board. Alas, not all passengers were scrupulous. The Pullman Company found card sharks frequenting cars at such an alarming rate during the twenties that it posted signs warning, "Passengers can protect themselves by refusing to play with strangers."

Besides collecting railroad paper and hardware, many rail buffs love to photograph trains and have extensive collections of both black-and-white and color photos showing all phases of railroading. Some prefer depots and stations, others bridges or locomotives.

The Railroad Enthusiasts, Incorporated, has been bringing together people interested in early railroading since 1935. As Mrs. J. W. Atherton, Secretary for the Railroad Enthusiasts put it, "When the group started we met at the Back Bay Station in Boston. As the club grew larger, we began meeting at hotels. At the present time we have 12 divisions from the East Coast to the West Coast, with a total membership of 1400." The original group, now called the Massachusetts Bay Division, today encompasses 350 members alone. Membership in the group costs only $3 a year, and those interested should write to Mrs. Atherton at the Railroad Enthusiasts, Incorporated, P.O. Box 133, West Townsend, MA 01474.

What's ahead for railroadiana? As one dyed-in-the-wool rail fan said, "The hobby's grown tremendously over the years; this trend is bound to continue as more and more people get aboard and awaken others to the magic of our railroad heritage."

He was wearing a conductor's cap when he said that. □ □

Automobilia

Even if you can't afford a Duesenburg . . .

Harper's Weekly, *July 22, 1899, captioned the above photo "Across the continent by automobile — Mr. and Mrs. Davis soon after starting, attended by friends."* Right: *Official New Hampshire Motor Guide (1927) and Amoco's 1943 tours of Boston.*

W HO collects automobilia? Of course, many of the people who collect old automobiles also collect their accessories, but as one put it, "Collecting automobilia is the perfect solution for those of us who love the early days of the American automobile, but find a 1921 Stutz Bearcat beyond our reach."

The prices of vintage cars, like everything else, have gone sky-high over the past decade (see inset). With original cars increasingly expensive to acquire, people are turning to the more accessible souvenirs of early motoring, such as literature, maps, magazine advertisements, radiator emblems, headlights, horns, hubcaps, license plates, even gasoline pumps!

Although there is not at present day any association devoted to the collection of automobilia per se, there are a number of organizations centered around collection of antique autos, which, of course, are also concerned with the accessories for these autos. Most collectors belong to either or both of the two leading antique automobile organizations — the Antique Automobile Club of America and the Veteran Motor Car Club of America. "Our membership is currently 45,000 and includes all of the United States and fifty foreign countries in our ranks," William Bomgardner, manager of the Antique Auto Club of America, informed me. He adds that his group, founded in 1935, is the largest and oldest automotive historical society in the country. The annual convention is held each year in February in Philadelphia, Pennsylvania. The AACA's official publication, *Antique Automobile,* is

EIGHT EXAMPLES OF HOW VINTAGE CARS HAVE APPRECIATED IN VALUE

- 1911 Maxwell. *Model AB brass roadster, sometimes called Jack Benny's car because of the late comedian's fondness for it. It was restored to original mint condition, but most investors don't consider it prime auto to appreciate in price. Sold in the 1960's for $2,600 but would now bring around $12,000.*

- 1921 Hispano-Suiza. *One of the few cars ever turned out in Spain, and the only really great car the country ever produced. Has become exceedingly rare, since production ceased in the early 1930's. Considered the equal of Rolls Royce in engineering and design, there are only a handful in the U.S. Sold in early 1960's for $4,500 but is now worth $85,000.*

- 1927 Type 35B Bugatti. *Grand Prix chassis, built by Jean Bugatti himself, very advanced styling, with body-flow design considered unequalled even today. Has an eight-cylinder single-overhead-cam engine with supercharger. Sold in the 1960's for $5,200; now costs $100,000.*

- 1932 Duesenberg. *Model J convertible sedan with a Dietrich body. Has one of the last Duesenberg engines ever made (in about 1937) as a replacement for original engine. The body was completely replaced by a coach builder at the request of the owner. In early 1960's sold for $9,500. Today it is worth around $150,000.*

- 1932 Auburn Boat Tail Speedster. *Model 100 A, a two-seater, completely restored, with every nut and bolt cadmium plated. Car is yellow with red trim, has won many prizes at exhibitions. Sold in early 1960's for $6,500, but today is worth $80,000.*

Radiator ornaments, from top to bottom: stallion from Humber Pullman limousine (early '30's); kestrel from 1935 Riley; 1936 Jaguar.

issued bimonthly to members and contains a wealth of early automobile stories, photos and news events. The AACA has its headquarters at 501 West Governor Road, Hershey, PA 17033. The Veteran Motor Car Club of America, whose members are similar in interest to those comprising the AACA, has its mailing address in care of the Secretary, 105 Elm Street, Andover, MA 01810. The bimonthly publication of this club is titled *The Bulb Horn*.

Other organizations in this field include Auto Enthusiasts International (Box 31A, Royal Oak, MI 48068) and The Horseless Carriage Club of America (9031 East Florence Avenue, Downey, CA 90240).

The largest of the many categories making up the field of automobilia today is literature. This includes sales materials, operator's manuals, tour books and road maps. Service-station road maps as we know them first came along in the mid-1920's. Before that time maps were printed in the *Automobile Blue Book*, the "bible" of early motorists. The maps in these books utilized existing landmarks for direction, as most of the first auto routes were

1927 Type 35B Bugatti.

- 1935 Rolls Royce. *The Phantom II convertible is an exceptionally rare type of Rolls with a six-cylinder overhead-valve engine. One of the former owners spent $5,400 just to restore the engine alone. Sold in the 1960's for around $7,500, but on today's market is worth around $50,000.*

- 1938 Mercedes-Benz. *540 K Convertible, Type A cabriolet two-seater, type of car built for higher ups in the Nazi party. Has an eight-cylinder overhead-cam engine and a five-speed transmission. Sold for $5,500 in '60's, worth $85,000 now.*

- 1951 Cad/Allard. *Good example of racing cars that made history in the 1950's. A fine touring sports car of English design with a Cadillac engine, can achieve speeds of 145 miles an hour. Sold then for $2,500, worth $18,000 now.*

(Courtesy of Alan D. Haas)

unposted. A New Hampshire *Blue Book* from the 1920's explained how to get from downtown Portsmouth to Manchester by car. "When you reach two-tenths of a mile at Middle Street and the library, turn left. At one and one-tenth miles there is a fork in the road. Bear right. Take the first right at the trolley tracks and continue out of town . . ." Copies of the *Automobile Blue Book* of the teens and early twenties sell for $8-$15.

One of the earliest manufacturers of road maps was the Mid-West Map Company of Aurora, Missouri. Their combined Vermont and New Hampshire map from 1921 showed a total of seven hundred miles of thoroughfare criss-crossing the two states — only sixty miles of which were paved! Road maps from the 1920-1930 decade are worth $2 to $6 in most cases.

Magazine advertisements showing early automobiles are very popular. Many collectors purchase hundreds of old magazines at a time, just to go through them and cut out the advertisements for cars, which they frame or mount in scrapbooks. An 1899 ad for the Winton Motor Carriage, which you could then buy for $1000,

Radiator ornaments, from top to bottom: gorilla with lantern; gryphon head, probably custom-made for a European nobleman; wistful walrus from circa 1920 Mors car.

Here is Distinction with Economy

EVERYONE knows that the carry-all days of bulk and extravagance in motor cars are passing.

The demand is for a really high-grade, compact, light-weight, good-looking, perfectly-balanced, rattle-proof, comfortable and economical motor car with rare ability to perform—and built to serve the owner satisfactorily over a period of years.

People who have driven the new Jordan Sedan tell us we have produced such a car.

Men who are weary of big bulky cars like its alertness—its lack of side sway.

Women who drive it experience that exhilarating thrill which comes with a sense of perfect control and easy motion.

Everyone appreciates its warmth, comfort, roominess and quiet good taste.

No one need feel cramped or crowded. There is plenty of head room.

Lines low and trim—rounded to relieve the eye, grown weary of square corners.

Provision is made for carrying an extra tire on the left-hand running board.

A large trunk, containing two full-size suitcases, is conveniently mounted at the rear. Bumpers front and rear, a combination stop and tail lamp and automatic windshield cleaner are standard.

You may have the new Sedan in the exclusive Crane Simplex, the only real permanent finish—or Jordan blue if desired.

JORDAN

JORDAN MOTOR CAR COMPANY, INC. CLEVELAND, OHIO

Clockwise from above: *Magazine ad for 1924 Jordan motor car; license-plate collection; "The Strip," '30's and '40's exhibit at the Museum of Transportation, Boston, Mass.; radiator emblems.*

boasted the car's ability to "reach a speed up to 18 miles an hour and remain under perfect control." A 1925 ad for the Hupmobile Eight, sold new for $1795, promised "hair-trigger acceleration from eight eager cylinders — buoyant, easy, dashing — a mighty flood at the point of your toe!"

Magazine ads for early autos are usually sold in groups, as practically any magazine published fifty years or more ago offered at least a half dozen such ads. The July 1906 issue of *American Monthly Review of Reviews,* for example, carried seven auto ads. Most valuable are those promoting types of automobiles only briefly on the market. Four ads for the 1910 White Star Gasoline Car (a short-lived luxury item featuring an aluminum body and hand-buffed leather seats) can be worth $8, or about as much as twelve Rambler ads of the same period.

The earliest issues of motor magazines started around 1900 are high on many collectors' lists, including *Motor, The National Magazine of Motoring,* and *The Automobile,* published by the E.L. Powers Company of New York and described by its editors as "an original, high-class journal for automobilists." These magazines are collected uncut for their reference value and the information they contain on early automobiles.

Radiator emblems are currently in demand among collectors, fetching prices from $4 to $15, depending on condition. These emblems, which disappeared from American cars in the mid-1930's, were the metal logos found on the front of the radiator. Emblems taken from old Fords and Chevrolets can be obtained at flea markets for as little as $5 apiece, while emblems from classic cars like the Pierce Arrow are priced considerably higher. Along the same line are radiator ornaments, which crowned the hoods of many cars during the teens and twenties. Radiator ornaments are tagged at from $25 to $100, with those depicting human or animal figures ("mascots") going for the highest prices.

Even old hubcaps are finding a growing market among early auto collectors. So much so, in fact, that these collectors have banded together to form their own association, The Hubcap Collector's Club (Box 54, Buckley, MI 49620). Formed by Dennis Kuhn four years ago, the group has attracted members from all corners of the country. "Most collectors in our group try to secure at least one cap from each of the various makes of cars," Mr. Kuhn said. Collectors entering this field can find themselves easily overwhelmed by the numbers of hubcaps manufactured over the years. According to Kuhn, there have been over twenty-five hundred makes of cars produced in this country alone, each with its own distinctive hubcaps. The club newsletter, *The Hubcap Collector,* is "available to full-fledged members."

Radiator ornaments, top to bottom: crystal bird from 1930 Red Ashay; Pontiac; signed Lalique crystal from France.

One of the most attractive branches of automobilia is automotive brass. Until 1913, brass was found decorating most cars on the road, used in headlights, radiators, horns and carbide generators. The largest producer of brass lamps was the Gray & Davis Company of Amesbury, Massachusetts. The company turned out hundreds of lamps used on all makes of cars. The old headlamps

Gas-pump globes.

were run by gas, while the side lanterns and tail lights burned kerosene. This went out in 1913, when electricity was introduced to automobiles. A good pair of brass headlights today will sell for anywhere from $150 to $250.

One problem with collecting automotive brass is that much of it turns up cracked, which diminishes its value, as there is little chance of repair once a brass lamp has cracked.

Also sought are the old brass bulb horns (which predate electric horns) for their nostalgic sound and eccentric forms. Particularly popular are the double- and triple-twist horns.

Other alluring collectibles are the vanity flower vases which graced the interiors of the grand old deluxe cars of the earlier part of this century. These fitted into back-seat window mounts in the big closed limousines of the period. Some vases were made of cut glass, others of pressed glass or carnival glass. Rarely found in cars made after 1930, these regal reminders of the early days of motoring today currently fetch from $20 to $30. Old gear shift knobs, which were in fact large swirled agates in different color combinations, also entice; values here start at $25.

A number of years ago Americans were singing "You can trust your car to the man who wears a star — the big, red Texaco star." Today that Texaco star, along with all sorts of other service station memorabilia — advertising signs, gas globes, pumps, tools, glass bottles — constitute one of the largest fields of automobilia. A number of collectors have literally constructed entire service stations right in their own garages and basements. The huge gas pumps are desired by many collectors, although most limit themselves to one or two due to the size. These iron sentinels of the old hometown service station are now being sold for as much as $750 each. The globes which crowned the gas pumps of the pre-1940's preserved the name and trademark of the brand of gasoline dispensed by the service station — Socony, Tydol, Colonial Esso. Globes begin at $25.

All kinds of advertising signs from early service stations are being actively bought. Up until about World War II, most station signs were made of porcelain, and these are of particular interest. Prices of $75 to $150 are common for porcelain signs. The name of an automobile or service station brand on any piece of repair equipment instantly increases its value. As one collector explained, "A plain tire gauge is almost worthless in itself. But a

Riding the Rails and Hitting the Road/*Automobilia*

Tremont Street, Boston, circa 1925.

gauge labeled Buick, Sunoco or Ford has value as a collectible.''

Early oil cans and jars are collected, with jars being the more sought after of the two. Before cans came into use, motorists pulling into a service station asking for oil had it pumped from the barrel into a spouted glass bottle, which was used to pour the oil into the car's engine. These jars were embossed with brand names such as Koolmotor Oil or Champlin. Early oil jars sell for $8-$15, while cans seldom bring more than $10.

Ask any automobilia collector what the most popular field of auto-related antiques is and you'll invariably be told license plates. The Automobile License Plate Collectors Association (ALPCA) has over twelve hundred members. The group got underway in 1954 in North Attleboro, Massachusetts, but is now nationwide. ALPCA's information office is located in care of the Newsletter Editor, 161 East College Avenue, Westerville, OH 43081. The fabric of ALPCA is kept together by a constantly updated membership roster and a monthly newsletter which includes articles such as "License Plates in Brazil," "Plate Hunting With Metal Detectors" and "How To Display Plates," set amid scores of advertisements of interest to buffs.

Many license plate collectors attempt to acquire all the various United States "runs" (complete sets of plates from each state, from the earliest to the latest issue). The problem with this goal is that collections quickly run into thousands of plates and "you run out of space to store them." For this reason, many of the newer collectors entering the hobby choose to specialize in plates from just one state.

Unusual plates are of special interest as conversation pieces. One such plate is the 1948 glass-beaded marker from Connecticut, one of the first fully reflective plates. The series of brass plates issued by Maine in the late 1940's were an early attempt to combat rust. There are certain Florida plates that measure up to 16 inches across. Illinois issued plates made from soybeans between 1943 and 1948 because of the acute shortage of metal during the war. Large herbivorous animals such as deer and cattle found these plates very tasty!

The wide popularity of collecting early license plates can be attributed to the fact that plates are still numerous, and more are discovered every day. Plates turn up in abandoned garages, nailed to the roofs of sheds, or tiling the floors of dilapidated farmhouses.

Lithograph by Ernest Montaux.

The hobby has recently reached a new level of respectability — license plates are now actually being carried by antique shops.

License plates vary considerably in value from state to state. Populous states like New York have issued huge numbers of plates over the years, so that the supply of plates from such states available to collectors is abundant. Small states like Rhode Island and Delaware, where there are many fewer cars on the roads, issued fewer plates, so that less collectable stock exists for these states, and their plates are consequently more valuable.

All plates dating pre-1914 were produced during what is called by collectors "the porcelain era" and are rare. A 1908 Massachusetts porcelain plate is worth $30. A 1906 "First Year Porcelain" Pennsylvania plate recently sold for $125! Most plates from the 1920's, however, are currently valued under $10 each, with some worth no more than $2 or $3.

Collectors buying and selling in volume bring big prices into the picture. A complete set of the Louisiana series sold by an ALPCA member brought $1300. Much of the excitement of license-plate collecting lies in the continuing search for elusive plates to complete sets. In any given state series, there are at least one or two plates that collectors would love to get their hands on.

An important question to the automobilia collector is always "Where do you look?" Well, in common with most other collecting areas — auctions, ads in antiques or collectibles journals, antique shops, yard sales and the like. But you can save yourself hours of combing such sources if you are lucky enough to come across an old car beyond repair left to molder away in someone's field or barn. *That* is the automobile collector's gold mine! Buy it, tow it home, cut it all up, do a little fixing here, a little polishing there — and you'll have a small shopful of automobilia all at once — to keep, sell or trade, as you will.

The many fields of automobilia today constitute a large and expanding hobby which, as more cars gain the cherished title of "antique," will continue to broaden. For the vintage car buff, automobilia is a garage filled with headlights, horns and hubcaps. In one collector's words, "Automobilia is what's left over after a Duesenberg and a Model T meet head-on." □ □

Section 5

Grandma's Kitchen

Kitchen Utensils

Collectors' items? Yes, indeed . . .

AT one time or another, a tremendous variety of gadgets found their way into the American kitchen before the advent of electrical appliances — squeezers, pounders, grinders, rollers, holders, toasters, shakers, cookers, bakers — and somehow with their help, our grandmothers managed to create delicious treats to the tune of "Get 'em while they're hot!" Today old kitchen utensils are staging a comeback. Some are still useful, some are hopelessly outdated, and some never did work very well, but regardless, Grandma's "tools" are coveted by collectors preserving relics of our culinary past. Once again the cry is "Get 'em while they're hot!" But now we hear it at flea markets, auction blocks and antique shops.

According to one antique dealer, kitchen utensils are among the fastest selling items in the antique business. Unlike many antiques collected simply for show, kitchen utensils are often sought by people who aim to put them back to work in the modern kitchen. Recent sales of antique kitchen utensils indicate that the number of people desiring to emulate Grandma's cooking has increased strongly over the past ten years. As a result, not only are Grandma's pots, pans and silverware being collected, but also her Triple Motion Ice Cream Freezer, Universal Breadmaker, Enterprise Coffee Mill and Griswold Crispy Corn Stick Pan.

Products once the pride and joy of now defunct companies like Landers, Frary & Clark of New Britain, Connecticut, are at the top of many collectors' lists. The company was formed in 1862, when George Landers dissolved his hooks, locks and latches business to enter into the production of kitchen utensils, and went on to manufacture a vast diversity of kitchen gadgetry now much in demand by culinary collectors. Food scales, sausage stuffers and lemon squeezers rolled off the company's production

Grandma could buy these time-savers for $1.50 and $2.00 in 1900. Today they are worth at least ten times what she paid. As advertised in the Ladies' Home Journal, *1905, and* The Women's Home Companion, *1900.*

line nonstop. But it wasn't until 1890, when the tradename "Universal" was adopted, that the company's sales really soared.

The Universal Food Chopper was the first best seller. Supplanting the old chopping bowl and knife, it transformed unattractive odds and ends into tasty casseroles for the family. "Universal does away with drudgery!" the ads proclaimed, and suddenly the name was on the lips of every homemaker. A succession of hit sellers followed — including the Universal Coffee Percolator (heated on a stove and described as "the perfection of the drip process") and the Universal Breadmaker ("dough prepared in the evening rises overnight"). Though you could purchase a Universal Breadmaker for $2 in 1909, today be prepared to pay up to $20 for this item in fine condition.

The king of kitchenware in the Northeast, however, was Manning-Bowman Company of Meriden, Connecticut. Well over one million Manning-Bowman enamel tableware sets adorned the nation's dinner tables in the 1890's. Emerging in the 1830's as a tinware manufacturer, the company instituted one of the first successful networks of door-to-door salesmen. Tinware rattling against the sides of the wagon as a salesman pulled into town became a familiar sound throughout the region. But, by 1872 the wagons and tinware had disappeared; the company had changed over to mounted enamelware. The vogue for enamelware which dominated the late nineteenth century catapulted Manning-Bowman sales of tableware and chafing dishes.

Another top seller was the Manning-Bowman "Eclipse" bread kneader and mixer, publicized as an "up-to-date and economical household labor-saving device." Orders for the Eclipse came in at such a rate that a separate building had to be constructed solely for its manufacture.

Manning-Bowman enamelware could be purchased for $2 a set in 1886, but expect to pay more than that for each piece now. Check carefully before purchase, though, because enamelware has a tendency to chip, and pieces in collectable condition are rare.

Early aluminum kitchenware is also popular today, particularly pieces made in Sidney, Ohio, where the Wagner Manufacturing Company, already noted for its cast-iron hollowware, capitalized on the development of a method of separating the silvery metal substance from alum by electric current in the late 1880's. The company began in 1881 with a two-building factory which employed twenty people. By 1913, Wagner Manufacturing was a sprawling network of buildings employing over three hundred workers. The company had the aluminum market almost entirely to itself for a number of years, producing kitchenware made of the inexpensive new metal — aluminum coffeepots, kettles, roasters, saucepans and other products — by the thousands. Wagner was very secretive about its aluminum-producing process and installed a Fort Knox-like security system in the portion of the plant where the electrical alum-separating devices were housed. The company survives today, as a division of the General Housewares Corporation of Sidney.

While most company catalogues contained a huge selection of

Records Broken
Time and Quality

Two things are necessary to making good ice cream quickly.

The first is a WHITE MOUNTAIN FREEZER. Second is to know how.

Your dealer will sell you the freezer. We will send you *free* the book that tells how.

Ordinary freezers are seldom used because they make hard, disagreeable work, which becomes an easy, economical task with the

Triple Motion

White
Mountain
Ice Cream Freezer

The freezer with a character and reputation to sustain; the standard freezer of the world.

Write at once for a **FREE** *copy of the revised book,*
"FROZEN DAINTIES"

Contains trustworthy recipes for the best frozen desserts of all kinds and tells how to make them with least labor.

The WHITE MOUNTAIN FREEZER CO.
Dept. F, Nashua, N. H.

Above: *The lady is timing her ice-cream freezer.* Right: *Tin coffee grinder.* Below: *Assorted tin molds.*

kitchen products, one New Hampshire firm entered more homes than most by manufacturing a single very successful product — ice cream makers. When Grandma took out her Triple Motion White Mountain Ice Cream Freezer on a hot Sunday afternoon, you knew you were in for a treat. Resembling a wooden mop bucket with a Victrola crank mounted on its top, this clever contraption was the crowning achievement of an enterprising company located for many years in Nashua, New Hampshire.

Clockwise, from top: *Tin canisters, copper apple-butter kettle, early electric toaster, Victorian rolling pin and measuring cup.*

The freezer possessed two tubs, the larger outside tub of pine and a smaller inside one made of tin. Salt and ice were poured in the space between the two while the small tub (containing a beater system) was filled with cream. When the crank was turned, the inside tub rotated and the cream was vigorously mixed by the beaters. And, *voilà!* ice cream in 30 minutes. The White Mountain Ice Cream Freezer had its share of competitors, among them Polar Star, American, Peerless Iceland, Blizzard, Jack Frost and Gem. If you're lucky enough even to find a pre-1900 model, you'd better plan on selling a lot of ice cream to make your profit. They've been known to run into the hundreds of dollars.

Kettles are perhaps *the* most popular item in the field of kitchen collectibles today. Tea kettles, cooking kettles, doughnut kettles, fish kettles — the more unusual the kettle, the more desirable it is. Early goosenecked tea kettles are much sought because of their interesting design. Some of the earliest kettles now go for up to $75; an eighty-year-old Wagner cast-iron doughnut kettle is worth $35. In caring for iron kettles, do not attempt to remove rust with an electric sander, as this will pit the iron. Instead, remove the rust by hand with steel wool; then rub in a small amount of oil with a soft cloth to restore the surface.

Wrought iron is substantially higher priced than cast iron. Early wrought-iron toasters surviving from the middle nineteenth century are usually priced at between $25 to $75 by antique shops. Wrought-iron and cast-iron mechanical utensils also command premium prices. Perhaps the most impressive are old coffee mills. The Enterprise Manufacturing Company of Philadelphia turned out the widest selection — everything from single-wheel counter models to the large two-wheel floor models. Painted red, white and blue with an American eagle crowning the whole affair, the Enterprise Number 5 was a spectacular piece of mechanical craftsmanship. Elaborate coffee mills like this today run from $200 to $400 or more.

Clockwise from upper left: Lemon squeezer, footed pan, spice grinder, wooden ewer, spice box, horn lantern, reflector oven, sugar-loaf breakers, toaster, wooden utensils, and a soup skimmer.

Careful housewives used scales to check that food purchased was full weight.

Early pewterware. On tray — large porringers surrounded by set of graduated measuring cups and a small funnel. Inset — complete place setting with snuff box (far left).

Glowing copper enriches any collection. Few fine pieces of kitchen copper are actually in use now, as most collectors prefer to keep their polished copper utensils on display. Copper molds are most decorative hung on kitchen walls. These molds were made in many different shapes and sizes. Molds designed for puddings, cakes, ice cream and candy can be found in the shapes of hearts, spades, fish, Kewpie dolls, rabbits, and countless other patterns. Regular cleaning with buttermilk will keep your copper dazzling.

Copper prices too are high. A 10-inch tin-lined copper saucepan with an iron handle, made in Duparquet, New York, in the 1850's, was recently listed in a dealer's catalogue for $85! Old copper teakettles sell for $40-$50 or more; a 1904 Manning-Bowman model with a brass spout and wooden handle brought $48. An early copper apple-butter kettle, if you can find one, would certainly cost at least $80-$100.

Antique woodenware is hard to date reliably because utensils such as bowls, chopping boards, butter spades, rolling pins, etc. were rarely marked by their manufacturers. Thus it is hard to tell an eighty-year-old chopping bowl from one produced today. The heft of the wood may provide some indication of age, because lighter wood is used in modern products. The color is also a clue since maple, oak and pine all darken evenly with age.

Undoubtedly the woodenware items most in demand are old rolling pins. The earliest pins are mostly plain and made of very heavy, solid wood. More intricate ones came later (including some made of blown glass). Prices for wooden rolling pins from the mid-nineteenth century average between $20 and $30. Old wooden breadboards from the late 1800's sell for $10-$20. Most chopping bowls which can be authenticated to date from the nineteenth century run from $30 to $40, but a 10-inch bowl made in 1840 of New Hampshire burl walnut sold not long ago at a Massachusetts flea market for $225. A wooden milk pitcher measuring only 5 inches high and marked Lockport, New York, 1883, went for $20. Clearly, it is well worth the woodenware collector's time to look around!

Every collector hopes to acquire at least one fine piece of pewterware for his collection, but this is becoming increasingly difficult. As one collector said, "You can hardly touch the stuff today — even the smallest plate!" Kitchen pewter included drinking cups, mugs, porringers, spoons, forks, saltboxes — anything that you wouldn't put over direct heat. At one time pewter was viewed as a cheap metal, owing to the fact that it melted easily. But as pewter utensils age, they acquire a beauty all their own, and this patina* has helped send the price of pewter items through the roof. Take, for example: a 12-inch coffeepot made in 1830 by the Allen Porter Company of Maine — $400; an 1840's pewter funnel — $45; a spoon crafted by Luther Boardman of Chester, Connecticut, in the 1830's — $50; a 1793 porringer with a trefoil handle and marked David & Thomas, Melville, Rhode Island — $1700! Prices are high even on late pewter — a five-piece tea and coffee set with rosewood handles made in the 1920's is valued at $140.

If you feel a little underfinanced at this point, take heart and consider galvanized kitchen tin, at the other end of the spectrum. For collectors planning to use their prizes, a box of early twentieth century tinware is a dream come true — ladyfinger pans, muffin tins and cookie cutters "just like Grandma's." True, such a purchase is more useful than profitable, due to the enormous quantity of tin items produced early in this century. Galvanized tin can be fun, however. One can hope to pick up a marvelous assortment of parers, jaggers, scoops, corers and measuring spoons for no more than $5. But don't ever pass up examples of real handmade tinware from the nineteenth century. These items, unlike their galvanized successors, are quite valuable. Old handmade cookie cutters are worth up to $25 and large advertising tins often bring $50-$100.

What makes yesterday's kitchen utensils so popular today? It's sort of like asking why hand-cranked ice cream, freshly baked bread and Grandma's homemade apple pies were so popular. Is this the advent of a trend to supercede the microwave kitchen? Hardly. But move over, Tupperware — iron, copper, pewter, wood and tin are definitely back! □ □

*Although some collectors prefer to let their pewter age naturally, others choose to clean it regularly with a paste made of powdered wood ash, salt, and vinegar.

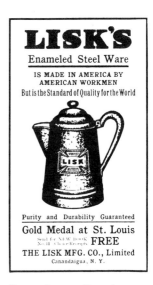

Enamelware first became popular during the 1870's. This ad is from a 1905 Ladies' Home Journal.

Wood Stoves

The useful *antiques that are coming back into their own . . .*

WOOD stoves are not exactly your everyday collectible. For years following the introduction of oil as cheap and plentiful (!) fuel requiring a minimum of effort, the ungainly cast-iron giants were sold as scrap. Replaced by oil furnaces and gas and electric cook stoves, woodburning stoves became increasingly unwelcome in the twentieth century home. Sportsmen told of picking up antique stoves for camps and cabins for a song. But that all changed during the early seventies when the new term "fuel shortage" entered our language. Suddenly Grandma's old Home Comfort range looked pretty good to a whole new generation of Americans who were coming to grips with the baffling world of flues, fireboxes and stovepipe. No longer are wood stoves picked up for a song. Prices now range from $100 to $500; a few exceptional examples, such as early Franklin or rare soapstone stoves, may command over $1000.

Wood stoves differ from other antiques in that most of those collected are put into actual use. Except for museum pieces, most stoves sold at auction are destined for service. Hardware stores confirm this by reporting an increase in the number of people purchasing stovepipe. Few people buy more than a stove or two at most, placing an emphasis on quality rather than quantity. One buys an antique stove as one would a fine piece of old furniture.

Woodburning kitchen ranges outprice parlor and box stoves three to one, as they always have, being the largest and most complex members of the wood stove family. While early Glenwood parlor stoves bring from $160 to $175 in good condition, a Glenwood C cookstove with six lids fetches $300 and a Glenwood E range with black finish and nickel trim, $450 to $500. A Round Oak cookstove now sells for $325, a Crescent for $275, and the attractive gray and white enamel Home Comfort range, made by the Wrought Iron Range Company of St. Louis, Missouri, for $300.

Condition is an important consideration in the purchase of an old stove. There should be no cracks caused by heat or wear in the stove surface or firebox. It is very difficult to repair cracks in a wood stove. There are several cement caulking compounds on the market, but most last only a short while. Only a professional ironsmith can fully repair a stove, and this can be expensive.

The highest priced stoves, for the most part collected only for display, are those produced in America during the 1700's and early 1800's. Benjamin Franklin designed his first stove as early as 1742. Early Franklin stoves were made of heavy cast iron and designed to be right within the fireplace. Because of the greater radiating surface of the cast iron, heat from the Franklin stove was

In 1908, Sears, Roebuck & Co. advertised a range whose entire top plate could be lifted so the cook could lay the fire evenly — and broil steaks too!

A handsome example of Francestown's famous soapstone box stoves in the Francestown, N.H., Historical Society.

retained for much longer after the coals had cooled down than was possible with a fire on the hearth. Sun-ray patterns were a trademark of the first Franklins, but the design also appears on contemporary stoves of this kind made by others. During this period, there was a certain degree of pattern variation, as others attempted to improve on Franklin's original design. Variations increased considerably as stove production entered the nineteenth century.

Box stoves came into vogue in the early 1800's as iron foundries sprang up all across the country. The first box stoves sat on stands 12 to 14 inches high. Small stoves used in bedrooms were called "four o'clock stoves" because that was the time they were usually lit. Beginning in 1809, stoves were manufactured in Francestown, New Hampshire, from locally quarried soapstone; their iron frames were produced at a foundry in nearby Peter-

Clockwise from top left below: *Stove featuring an elevated oven; Portland Stove's Atlantic Parlor Stove; cast-iron fireplace invented in 1742 by Benjamin Franklin; Atlantic cookstove without reservoir (one could be attached).*

Traveling case (above) for salesman's soapstone-stove sample (right). Stove legs are detachable. The case is metal and stands approximately 16 inches high.

Below: Two flues instead of one were used in this 1840 two-column stove. The cylinder above radiated heat into the room.

borough. Soapstone stoves resembled the Franklin fireplace stoves, but had the added advantage of holding the heat for hours longer. Soapstone is gray, very soft, and has a somewhat greasy feel. Incredibly heavy, these stoves were ferried by ox cart to merchants in Boston (it took three days). There, many were loaded on ships for sale in ports around the world. A number of very beautiful examples can be seen today in museum collections. The last soapstone stove I saw on the market stood about four feet high, was encased in an ornate iron frame, and bore a tag of $800.

The workhorses of the stove family, the cast-iron ranges, introduced Victorian splendor into the kitchen with their elaborate, often magnificent, cast work. Mid-nineteenth century manufacturers touted their products vigorously, advertising in glowing hyperbole: "None Other On Earth Can Compare to its Superiority in Capacity, Convenience, and Heating Comfort!"; "The Very Highest Grade of Cooking Stove Ever Made"; "You Have Got To Have the New Fairmount!"; "Barstow! Barstow! Refuse All Else!"

The pride of such companies were their "showcase" models — cast-iron works of art, festooned with shiny silver nickel trim. Models like the Britannia Special, the Empress Atlantic, and The Commonwealth were impressive examples of nineteenth century castmolding. Competition led to more and more extravagant examples of the stovemaker's art, sometimes verging on the bizarre. Rivalry likely reached its zenith when the Richmond Stove Company of Norwich, Connecticut, manufacturers of the popular Richmond Range, Farmer's Stove, and Triumph, unveiled "The most ornate stove in the world" at the Cincinnati Exposition in the autumn of 1873. The most ultra of ultra-deluxe models, it was indeed a sumptuous stove. From the base of its legs to the top of the mantel, the Grand Palace Range glistened silver all over, covered completely with highly polished nickel plating. Em-

Below: *The elaborately cast Atlantic Oak burned either wood or coal.* Right: *This sturdy Glenwood double-oven, double-flue range is still in regular use.*

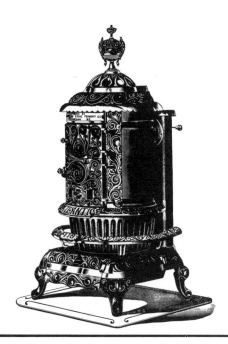

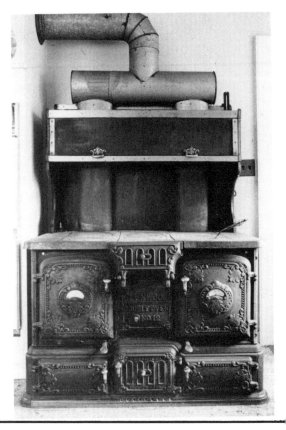

bellished with intricate raised castwork of remarkable detail, this single stove took more than twenty skilled molders an entire year to create. The metal masterpiece toured the country in its own boxcar during 1874 and 1875, attracting throngs wherever it went.

One of the most widely distributed models was the Kalamazoo, a line of mail-order woodburners advertised by the catchy phrase, "A Kalamazoo Direct To You." The Michigan company first presented its steel- and nickel-trimmed ranges and parlor stoves in 1902. They became immediate sales phenomenons thanks to a vigorous advertising campaign which proclaimed in all the nation's leading publications: "We will send you, freight prepaid, direct from our factory, any Kalamazoo stove or range on a 360 days approval test." "We guarantee our product under a $20,000 bank bond." Thousands of Kalamazoos were sold during the first years of the company's existence; the slogan, "A Kalamazoo Direct To You" was to go down in American advertising history.

Few companies produced a more popular line of wood stoves than the Weir Stove Company of Taunton, Massachusetts. Founded in 1878, Weir scored initial successes with models like the Hudson, Sunrise, Crescent, Old Colony and Fleetwood.

Grandma's Kitchen/*Wood Stoves*

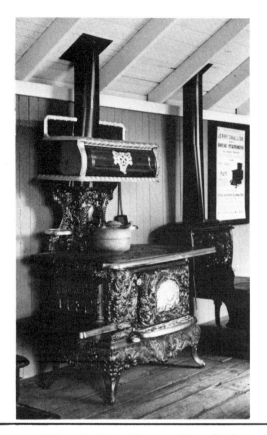

Left: *Fancy nickel-trimmed stove with high warming closet and coffee and teapot stands below high shelf.* Right: *A reservoir range (reservoir on right in this picture).*

Although these lines sold well, it was the introduction of the Glenwood around 1900 that brought the Taunton company world recognition. These somewhat ordinary-looking stoves appealed strongly to the homemaker, being easy to operate and not requiring much attention. Their very lack of ornamentation made them easier to keep spruce.

Advertised shortly as the "Popular Glenwood," the stove outsold and continued to outsell all others in the Weir line. By 1920 the company was manufacturing and distributing only the Glenwood in variations of the original design — the Glenwood "D," "S," "C" and so on. All were very popular.

Glenwood models fell into two categories: square ranges and reservoir ranges. The square models sold better in urban areas, while reservoir ranges were popular down on the farm. Reservoir ranges had a special receptacle built on to hold water, which would be heated and kept hot by the fire within the stove. The square stoves had no such receptacle. The Glenwood "C" was listed in the 1916 catalogue at $58.00 for the square style and $76.50 for the reservoir range. The purchaser was offered a choice of a single-mantel shelf, double-mantel shelf, or warming closet. All three options came delivered, complete with 6-inch black stovepipe.

The company also made cast-iron Glenwood wood-burning parlor stoves in three sizes, priced between $20 and $26. Manufactured during the spring and summer months, they were generally sold out by the first of October. The company melted tons of scrap iron daily and employed 240 molders.

In July, 1926, Thomas Slattery went on the road as a salesman for the Taunton firm, by then known as the Glenwood Range Company. He recalls a visit to President Calvin Coolidge's Vermont home. Both the kitchen range and parlor stove were Glenwoods! "The 'Glenwood' parlor stove was in the small room where he was sworn in as President, and it showed up in all the press pictures." It was about that time that Mr. Slattery saw his first electric range, in Rutland, Vermont, part of a Hotpoint appliance display.

As America entered the 1930's, the woodburning stove was on the way out. Advertisements in *Good Housekeeping* and *The Ladies Home Journal* exhorted the housewife to "Cast Aside Those Iron Monsters! Move up to the 20th Century." Oil, gas, and electricity, all in plentiful supply, were the coming thing. One after another, the old brands of stoves began to disappear from the catalogues. The Glenwood Company produced its last new woodburning parlor stoves in the spring of 1930. Glenwood kitchen ranges were manufactured through 1938. The Kalamazoo Stove Company, unable to adapt to the changing times, was liquidated in 1952, by which time Americans were almost exclusively heating and cooking with oil, gas, or electricity. The wood stove faded into a memory.

And that's about the way things stayed until the seventies, when it became apparent that supplies of fossil fuels were not unlimited — indeed were fast becoming limited. Traditional sources of energy were rediscovered. For many, wood energy was an answer. Interest in the "iron monsters" of the past sprang up almost overnight. Old stoves were swept up wherever they could be found, and modern reproductions of the original Franklins, box stoves, parlor stoves and kitchen ranges sold fast.

As fine as the new remakes are, most people will agree that nothing compares to an original wood stove for quality and efficiency. This is understandable. A century ago, wood-stove production was a craft. Today it is a business. With more and more people turning to wood heat, today's collector now not only is competing with other collectors for the dwindling supply of original wood stoves, but also with the general public. And this ever-increasing market continues to drive up prices.

In these days of fuel shortages, families with a wood stove and a full woodshed can be assured of a warm house all winter and scoff at power failures. The wood stove is reclaiming its place in the mainstream of family life. Just as before, it warms and dries rows of socks and mittens on winter evenings, sits in on conversations around the dinner table, and brings forth all kinds of treats for the holidays. Many are discovering all over again for themselves that there *was* something special about Grandma's old stove! □ □

Section 6

When You and I
Were Young

Radio Memorabilia

Treasures once worth only a boxtop or two

"**A** cloud of dust, a galloping horse with the speed of light, a hearty Hi-Yo Silver! — The Lo-one Ranger!" How clearly those words evoke the stirring strains of the "William Tell Overture," keeping pace with the thunder of hooves as the Masked Man set out over the great radio prairie in swift pursuit of wrongdoers each Monday, Wednesday and Friday evening in the early 1940's. Meanwhile, "Buck Rogers in the 25th Century," radio's greatest interplanetary super-hero, rocketed to the farthest reaches of the Universe weekdays at 6:00 P.M. over CBS radio in a quest for outer space law and order, on behalf of that favorite earth food, Coco-Malt. For a Coco-Malt inner seal and a thin dime, anyone could qualify as an official "Buck Rogers Solar Scout" and pursue Martians wherever they were to be found in the community.

Anyone could become a super-hero. Just look at Lamont Cranston, a mere "wealthy man about town," or Clark Kent, an obscure "mild-mannered reporter" for the *Daily Planet.* Average

Charlie McCarthy as (above) a clock and (right) a cardboard puppet.

Bottom: *Orphan Annie memorabilia, including Little Orphan Annie's Song* (1933), *decoders, rings, and other items. After 1933, the radio show heroine was known as "Radio Orphan Annie" to differentiate her from the "Little Orphan Annie" still star of Harold Gray's comic strip.* Left: *A page in a Radio Orphan Annie Secret Society manual.* Below: *Annie's shake-up mug with Sandy and Annie figurines.*

A wind-up toy "Amos and Andy Fresh Air Taxicab."

citizens by day, but through the magic of radio, Lamont proved regularly that as the mysterious "Shadow," he alone knew "what evil lurks in the hearts of men," while the mild-mannered reporter soared nightly over Metropolis, fighting crime as "Superman." During the thirties and forties, listeners all across the country tuned in with eager anticipation to each continuing episode of these and other imaginative radio shows.

Although those golden days of American radio drama have long since ended, old radio memorabilia are today important collectibles. Radio premiums and give-aways and other radio-related items such as radio character watches, "Big Little Books," and vintage comic books based on radio serials fetch amazing prices, as collectors, striving for complete sets, will pay the top dollar merely to obtain "this Jack Armstrong," or "that Green Hornet."

One of the finest collections in the country has been assembled by Carl Terison, Jr., of Cumberland, Maine. He has spent the past decade amassing a dazzling array of radio serial memorabilia — badges, decoders, rings, whistles, detection kits, invisible ink pens — practically the entire range of radio premium offers of the thirties and forties. Initially a coin collector, Mr. Terison felt that the coin-collecting field was becoming overrun by experts, so about ten years ago he turned to radio premium collecting. He is the proud owner of a Shadow Blue Coal Ring, a nearly complete set of Radio Orphan Annie manuals spanning 1933 to 1940, and a mint condition Tom Mix Postal Signal Set. Originally available for only two Ralston box tops, the signal set is now a $40 investment.

The fragile radio premiums are somewhat difficult to locate. Radio Orphan Annie and Tom Mix items are the most common, as they had the largest original distribution. Hardest to find today are those from the Captain Midnight, Buck Rogers, Green Hornet, Lone Ranger and The Shadow shows, particularly paper items. Collector Terison explained why radio-related paper is so rare. "So much paper went for the huge paper drives of World

War II that very little radio-related paper survived to the post-war era. The items that did are few and those that do turn up are rarely in mint condition."

One treasure much sought by collectors is the detailed Radio Orphan Annie map. This rare, full-color map displays a bird's-eye view of Orphan Annie's hometown, Simmons Corner, showing everything from the village train depot to the Silo Farm, which Annie called home. This paper gem is valued at over $100. Another desirable, if rare, item is an original Charlie McCarthy Clock, made by the Gilbert Toy Company of New Haven, Connecticut, in 1938. Also of interest to today's collector are Dick Tracy and Orphan Annie wristwatches (worth $40-$50), made by the defunct New Haven Clock Company, and the famous Buck Rogers Pocket Watch, created by the Ingraham Company of Bristol, Connecticut, in 1935.

Big Little Books, which first appeared about 1933, published by the Whitman Company of Racine, Wisconsin, and the Saalfield Company of Akron, Ohio, were often written around popular radio characters and their shows. Whitman and Saalfield issued a long list of action-packed titles such as *Dick Tracy and the Man With No Face, Buck Rogers and the Fiend of Space, The Story of Edgar Bergen and Charlie McCarthy,* and *Captain Midnight and the Secret Squadron.* Some editions were equipped with an added attraction called "thumb movies." In the corner of each page of these little books was a small picture in a box. When the pages were flipped rapidly with the thumb, they provided a realistic miniature "movie."

Generally speaking, these soft-cover books, which measured about 4½ inches by 3½ inches and cost 5¢ (later upped to 10¢) each, presently sell for $4-$8 a copy. Flash Gordon, Buck Rogers and Dick Tracy editions are higher-priced, averaging as much as $10 to $15 for copies in reasonably good condition. A copy of *Flash Gordon and the Red Sword Invaders,* however, recently sold

Some of Carl Terison's extensive collection of Tom Mix premiums — badges, books, gadgets of use to a cowboy hero.

for $31. Lone Ranger and Green Hornet Big Little titles from the 1930's in mint condition are priced at $15-$20, and Little Orphan Annie books of the same vintage and condition, may bring up to $35 each.

Good hunting grounds for radio premiums are junk shops, flea markets and yard sales. Sometimes antique shops will have small dishes, ashtrays, or empty candy boxes overflowing with small items such as tie clasps, buttons, old guitar picks, marbles, class pins and the like. It is here that collectors will on occasion discover a Lone Ranger membership ring, or Tom Mix simulated gold badge. Careful scrutiny often pays off, as collectors have told of purchasing for 25¢ memorabilia worth $10-$15.

Prices of early radio items are dictated by a number of factors. Usually the highest prices are paid by the radio memorabilia collectors themselves; dealers seldom pay more than fifty percent of what a collector will pay, hoping to resell items to collectors and

Captain Midnight items are among the hardest to find.

realize a profit. The condition of an item is very important. Does Tony the horse have an ear missing on your Tom Mix Ralston Straight Shooters badge? Does that Tom Mix Makeup Kit actually contain makeup? Collectors strive to acquire items which are as close to original condition as possible. They will often purchase inferior items as substitutes for a desired item until a better example can be found, but, for these lesser quality premiums and giveaways, pay only a fraction of what they would pay for the same items in top condition.

Prices affixed to radio memorabilia are constantly changing, as they are influenced by the vogues of the times. The increased interest in science fiction and outer space in the late seventies, as prompted by popular motion pictures, had a considerable impact on the market, sending the prices of the already high-priced original Buck Rogers and Superman items even higher. A like-new Buck Rogers pencil box from the early thirties was recently spotted sporting a $25 price tag in one antique shop. Buck Rogers Sonic Ray guns sell for over $30. And the now almost legendary

Club pins, rank-identification badges, and (right) Frank Buck Sun Watch complete with instructions.

1935 Buck Rogers Pocket Watch is valued at $400 in working condition. The widely distributed Radio Orphan Annie Shake Up Mugs seldom are priced higher than $10, while the hard-to-find Orphan Annie Secret Society manuals have sold for $25 to $50 apiece. Some memorabilia never seem to fall out of popularity; such is the case with the Jack Armstrong memorabilia. The Jack Armstrong telescope and pedometer will bring $10 each from a collector, while Jack's flashlight sells for closer to $15. And you say you'd like to add a Charlie McCarthy Radio Party Game (vintage 1938) to your collection? Be prepared to pay over $30, if you're lucky enough to find one.

Radio advertisers were constantly devising new methods of promoting their products. In this quest, sponsors of afternoon and early evening programs for youngsters came up with the radio give-away concept in the early 1930's. Often termed "cerealized adventures," backed as they were by cereal and breakfast-food

Lone Ranger items. Clockwise from top left: pedometer, deputy badge, Victory Corps lapel stud, story and flashlight, telescope, and pistol rings.

companies, each program offered the listener an opportunity to become an official member of its particular fan club. This entitled listeners to receive the official "simulated gold badge," ring, booklet, decoder, whistle and many other premiums and give-aways. All that was required was the box top or inner seal from a sponsor's product, 10¢ in coin and an unbounded appetite for breakfast foods. Programs such as *Jack Armstrong, the All-American Boy, Buck Rogers in the 25th Century, The Lone Ranger, The Shadow,* and *Captain Midnight* counted their members in the thousands. Dick Tracy's club even had a special girls' division. Fascinating gadgets such as the Jack Armstrong Ped-O-Meter, which measured distances walked, the Lone Ranger Official Flashlight Ring, Silver Bullet Ring, and Filmstrip Ring (with action slides of the Masked Man and Tonto) were produced by the tens of thousands. Wheaties' *Frank Buck Explorers Show* introduced the famous "glow-in-the-dark" give-aways, but it took the Green Hornet to popularize them with the Green Hornet Secret Compartment Ring, which in the dark gave off a brilliant blue glow, possibly meant to suggest the program's sponsor, Blue Coal. Blue Coal favored rings, it seems — should you be lucky enough to find one of The Shadow's Blue Coal rings today, your collection would be $225 the richer.

Superman statuette.

The "Tom Mix Ralston Straight Shooters" show, heard weekdays at 5:45 P.M. over NBC held first place in premium peddling, as to both number and variety of gadgets distributed. All Tom Mix premiums were offered during the program; Ralston put more advertising money into its gadgets than any other company at the time, reaching an all-time high in 1937-38. During this period, the top give-away offers included the membership ring bearing the legend "Ralston Straight Shooters" and the magnetic ring, for picking up small metal items fast — such as stray outlaw bullets. There was also the Look Around Ring, equipped with a miniature mirror which acted as a microperiscope (today valued at $11) and the Genuine Gold Ore Tom Mix Badge ($9 today).

The show advertised heavily in the local Sunday color funnies with strips usually showing a short Tom Mix adventure, in which the hero overwhelmed wrongdoers by using some ingenious piece of equipment like the Look Around Ring. At the end of the strip, you were told how you could "be the first kid on the block" to have this official gadget. They were all endorsed by Tom himself, saying (as in a 1937 published offer), "I'll send you a beautiful simulated gold badge just like mine Free for just one Ralston box top!" Similar offers included the Special Sun Watch and Postal Telegraph Signal Set (now a $24 item). Tom Mix always urged his

Below: *Photographed in 1922 at New England's first radio station located in Medford, Massachusetts.*

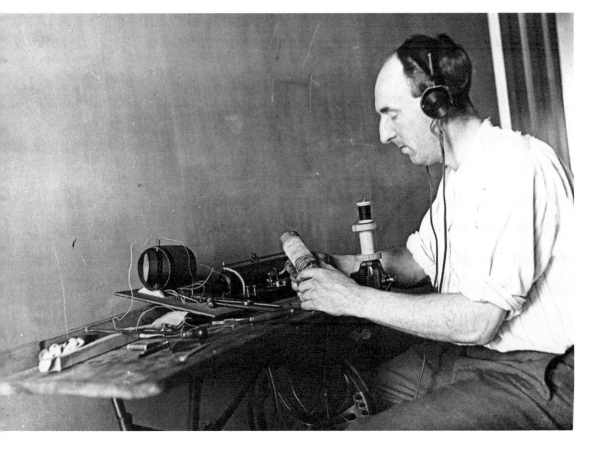

loyal fans to "hurry and get your Ralston tops to Checkerboard Square and fast, they won't last long," adding confidentially, "...and tell Mom about the nutritious value of Ralston breakfast cereals. I eat 'em every morning and you should too!"

Radio Orphan Annie was another of the highly successful product promoters. Orphan Annie, first heard nationwide in 1933 over NBC's red network, was none other than the famous character of comic serial fame, now getting into all sorts of trying and unlikely situations over the radio waves with her trusty dog Sandy. Sponsored during the 1930's by Ovaltine, in each broadcast Annie and Sandy set out to help those willing to accept the comforting words and worthy assistance of the little girl with blank-zero eyes. With Annie's help, Ovaltine established the record give-away in 1936. As Orphan Annie said, "Leapin' Lizards, Sandy! Now the boys and girls can enjoy the chocolate-flavored taste of Ovaltine in my new official 'Orphan Annie Shake-Up Mug'!" "That's right," the announcer would add, "it's Orphan Annie's very own Shake-Up Mug, yours for merely ten cents and the inner seal from a jar of Ovaltine." Within a matter of days the sponsor was literally swamped with Ovaltine seals and dimes. The offer was continued, and the envelopes continued to pour in. By mid-1938, it was estimated that the Orphan Annie mug sets adorned the breakfast table in more than a quarter of a million homes across the country.

Radio memorabilia collectors often augment their collections with recordings of actual radio programs. Mel Simons of West Roxbury, Massachusetts, a professional entertainer, has a library of close to fifteen thousand individual radio programs on tape.

Like many collectors, Mr. Simons first fell in love with radio as a youngster. "I was lucky enough to have been a kid in the late forties and early fifties, when many of these programs were still on the air," he explained. He managed to hold on to a few of the premiums from his childhood and has been adding to his collection ever since, which now includes about three hundred premiums ("I've had tremendous luck at flea markets").

Mel Simons is vice-president of a Massachusetts-based organization for early radio buffs, the Radio Collectors of America, started in 1971 to serve the New England area. Monthly meetings are held in Quincy, Massachusetts. (For more information, write to Radio Collectors of America, c/o Tom Kelly, 177 North Main Street, Andover, MA 01810.) At present there is no national group for radio memorabilia collectors. Other regional groups do exist — in New York and Baltimore, for example.

Older radio buffs see themselves preserving the memories of a form of entertainment which disappeared with the coming of television, but are delighted to find younger people entering the hobby — persons born in the television era with little personal recollection of old-time radio. Tapes have made it possible for this generation to come under the spell of the early radio shows just as their seniors did. They, too, know that the answer to that timeless radio question, "Who was that masked man?" is (of course) — "Why, that man was the Lone Ranger!"   □□

Baseball Cards

"Can a batter swing at the same pitch twice?"

The Big League in baseball cards is the fabled Honus Wagner card, now worth $3000+. Cards pictured center and right, by contrast, bring only $5 and $1, respectively.

TO the kids of the 1950's, they were the best buy in town. For the 5¢ you put down at the corner store, you received a pack of bubble gum containing the pictures of as many as ten Major League baseball players. With each new pack, your expectations soared — maybe it contained a Mickey Mantle, a Willie Mays or a Roy Campanella. Yes, maybe even a Ted Williams! This time you were lucky: "Theodore Samuel Williams, outfield, Boston Red Sox. Ted is one of the greatest hitters of all time," Topps card number 1 told us. "In '41 he hit .406. Named the Most Valuable Player in '46 and '49. He has the highest Lifetime Batting Average of any active player. Bats left. Throws right." Thumbing through your pack you quickly discover other "secrets." Yogi Berra's real first name is Lawrence. Pitcher Ed Roebuck of the Brooklyn Dodgers learned to throw by practicing knocking tin cans off a fence. Yankees' Phil Rizzuto was turned down by the Dodgers because he was too short (5 foot 6 inches). Packs of baseball cards constituted gold mines of information for the young sports fan. They told us everything we wanted to know — everything! "Can a batter swing at the same pitch twice?" asked Topps card 130 (picturing Phillies' Mayo Smith). Answer: "Yes, if he doesn't hit it the first time."

Baseball cards, around in one form or another for nearly a hundred years, are easy to collect, easy to store, and easy to identify. Their appeal is based primarily on the unmistakable nostalgia they generate for sports fans. "I can relate to baseball players much better than I can to coins or stamps," one dyed-in-the-wool enthusiast told me. "Looking at a Willie Mays card sends me back to the time I was a kid. It's great!"

Baseball cards first appeared in this country during the 1880's, issued by American tobacco companies in packs of cigarettes. Somebody had come up with the clever idea of reproducing pictures of personalities on the small pieces of cardboard inserted in cigarette packs to stiffen the package. Actors, actresses, politicians, generals and other celebrities of the period were commonly pictured as well as baseball players. But baseball was right there at the start. Firms like Goodwin & Company and Allen & Ginters assembled scores of early ball players before studio cameras to pose a swing in the name of their popular brands of cigarettes. Most of those pictured were obscure players whose only claim to fame in many cases was their appearance on a tobacco card. It would not be until long after the demise of tobacco cards that the greats of baseball were portrayed — Babe Ruth, Lou Gehrig, Joe DiMaggio, and the like. Today, these are the names that draw collectors. Consequently, despite their age, the earliest baseball cards are generally not worth as much as the latest counterparts issued from the 1930's through the 1950's by chewing-gum companies. A common tobacco card of the late nineteenth century has a price range competitive with that of 1930's bubble-gum cards. This is understandable in view of the fact that few people remember St. Joseph's player P. Flood, pictured on an 1885 "Old Judge" card issued by Goodwin & Company, whereas *everybody* remembers Leo Durocher, pictured on a Goudey "Big League" gum card in 1933. The recognition factor is important to the value of a card.

The cards below (left to right) were issued by Hassan Cigarette (now worth $1.25); C. A. Briggs (lozenge) Co., 1909 (valued at $10); and Playball (gum) Inc., 1941 ($20 value).

Most tobacco cards are priced at a few dollars apiece and usually run no higher than $10. The ten players in Allen & Ginters' "Champion" series (1888) are worth about $10 each. Goodwin's "Old Judge" cards issued in the 1880's sell for $6-$10.

There certainly are exceptions to this, however! Sooner or later baseball-card collectors get around to discussing the famous Honus Wagner tobacco card. The latest estimate of this single card's value runs over $3000. Honus Wagner, who played for Pittsburgh, did not use tobacco. When his picture was issued on a tobacco card, he became very indignant and threatened to sue unless distribution was stopped. Some cards were circulated before the company managed remand of the card, and to acquire one of these few is the aspiration of every baseball-card collector. Only about a dozen are known to exist today. The value of the Wagner card, or any valuable card for that matter, can fluctuate greatly, a collectible's worth being always what the highest bidder is willing to pay.

Bubble-gum companies first entered the baseball-card field around 1910. Leading companies over the years have been Goudey, DeLong, Bowman, Philadelphia Gum, Fleers, and Topps. The famous "bubble-gum-card war" of the early 1950's happened when two companies, Bowman and Topps, achieved nearly total domination of the market. Bowman had already been producing cards for a number of years when Topps entered the picture in 1951 with its first set of ninety-six cards. There was lively competition between the two firms as to which gave the

Topps, Inc.'s Hank Aaron card (below, center), the first to feature him, now sells for $50. Card on left ($5) folds out to show another player. A 1958 Topps card ($7) stars Willie Mays.

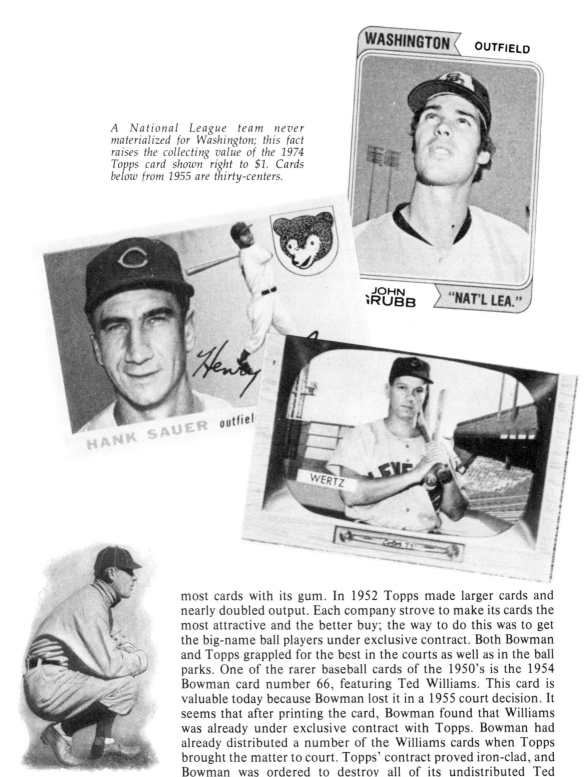

A National League team never materialized for Washington; this fact raises the collecting value of the 1974 Topps card shown right to $1. Cards below from 1955 are thirty-centers.

WASHINGTON OUTFIELD

JOHN GRUBB "NAT'L LEA."

HANK SAUER outfiel

WERTZ

most cards with its gum. In 1952 Topps made larger cards and nearly doubled output. Each company strove to make its cards the most attractive and the better buy; the way to do this was to get the big-name ball players under exclusive contract. Both Bowman and Topps grappled for the best in the courts as well as in the ball parks. One of the rarer baseball cards of the 1950's is the 1954 Bowman card number 66, featuring Ted Williams. This card is valuable today because Bowman lost it in a 1955 court decision. It seems that after printing the card, Bowman found that Williams was already under exclusive contract with Topps. Bowman had already distributed a number of the Williams cards when Topps brought the matter to court. Topps' contract proved iron-clad, and Bowman was ordered to destroy all of its undistributed Ted

Williams cards. (Surviving examples of this card have been known to sell for as much as $75.) By 1956 Bowman had disappeared, and only Topps remained on the market.

Baseball cards are graded according to condition. Understanding the various grades of cards is important, especially when dealing with other collectors through the mail. One collector's "mint" may be another's "very good." A system used by many collectors places cards into six grades: mint, excellent, very good, good, fair, and poor. An excellent-to-mint card has sharp corners. A good-to-very-good card can have rounded edges. A fair card may have corner damage, creases, and surface wear, while a poor card has water stains, gum stains and pin holes (many children tacked cards up on their walls). To keep cards from further depreciating, collectors mount them between plastic pages custom-made for baseball-card collectors. These are kept in loose-leaf notebooks.

Baseball-card collecting has seen its greatest increase as a hobby over the past ten years. The tremendous influx of new sports fans into the ranks of card-collecting has helped drive up the price of almost everything except for the very newest items. However, for the most part, cards from as late as the 1950's can still be bought for as little as 25¢ apiece. This may not sound like much until you realize that most collectors buy complete sets from dealers, and there are as many as 660 cards in a set. The number of cards issued yearly is staggering. With luck it would conceivably be possible to collect a set every year, but in addition to luck it would require a very considerable financial investment. To add to the confusion, card series are now issued that feature minor leagues — teams like the Bristol (Connecticut) Red Sox or the Fort Lauderdale (Florida) Yankees.

One publication which helps collectors keep abreast of the cavalcade of cards is *Sports Collectors Digest* (409 North Street, Milan, MI 48160), published twice monthly and filled with articles and advertisements pertaining to baseball-card collecting. The *Digest* started out as a folded three-page flyer. A typical issue now contains eighty pages, with a large classified section. The prosperity of this publication over the past decade mirrors the rapid growth of the sports collecting field in general.

An Amawalk, New York, publication, *Baseball Advertiser,* claims to have the largest readership in the field — "51,000 strong," says Mike Aronstein of Card Memorabilia Associates, Ltd., publishers of the *Advertiser,* "better than four times the circulation of all other sports-collectible publications combined." *Baseball Advertiser* consists solely of ads, placed by both small collectors and big-time dealers all over the country. Ads can be placed by writing *Baseball Advertiser,* P.O. Box 2, Amawalk, NY 10501. Another New York periodical for sports collectors is *The Trader Speaks,* started in 1968. Published monthly at 3 Pleasant Drive, Lake Ronkonkoma, NY 11779, it is sent to subscribers by first-class mail for a dollar a copy.

Also of interest to card collectors are card shows ranging from the national shows held yearly in New York and Los Angeles to regional shows like the one held in Nashua, New Hampshire,

every March. Sponsored by an enthusiast named Bill Dod, the Nashua show is put on for the benefit of a high-school athletics program. "We've attracted collectors from as far north as Nova Scotia and as far south as Pennsylvania," Dod told me. The show has expanded considerably since its beginnings in 1972. "That first year we had only 55 people at the show. Our most recent show drew a crowd of 1500. We charge $7.50 per table rented, but admission is free. Card shows in large cities such as New York and Chicago charge up to $20 for tables," Dod added.

At present (1979), there is no national association for baseball-card collectors, although one may materialize in the near future, according to rumors presently circulating among collectors. Such an organization could set uniform standards for collecting on a national basis and solve such problems as grading and pricing — currently matters of regional discretion. Nevertheless, there are many active regional groups; regular check of the pages of a publication such as *Sports Collectors Digest* could put you in touch with one in your area.

One of the largest and best-known regional groups is the Eastern Pennsylvania Sports Collectors Club in the Philadelphia area. "We got started in January of 1978," said Robert Schmierer, who, together with fellow collector Ted Taylor, heads the group. "Basically we were just a group of collectors here in the Philadelphia area who had been putting on card shows for a number of years. We decided it was time to band together as a group." Interest in the new group quickly spread, and soon applications for membership came from collectors outside Philadelphia. At latest count, the club has about 450 members from twenty different states. Big events are the two card shows held each March and September at the George Washington Motor Grove in Willow Grove, Pennsylvania, with over 150 dealer tables and a combined attendance of over thirteen thousand. The $5 annual membership fee of the club covers the newsletter, membership card, free admission to the card show and a discount on all dealers' tables. The address of the Eastern Pennsylvania Sports Collectors Club is P.O. Box 37, Maple Glen, PA 19002.

The scope of baseball-card collecting today is overwhelming. To talk with a full-fledged enthusiast is to hear mentioned hundreds of players long forgotten, to see thousands of once-discarded cards now treasured. But most of all it is to realize how truly dedicated card collectors are to the game of baseball. Card collectors don't merely collect baseball — they think, live, and breathe baseball. The cards epitomize the glamor of the game. The teams, the scores, and all those players — Dizzy Dean, Dixie Walker, Jackie Robinson, Stan Musial, Whitey Ford, Duke Snider, Roy Sievers, Hank Greenberg — as long as there are baseball-card collectors, these names will remain immortal.

There's a world of baseball excitement stored in those gum wrappers: color photos of baseball stars, facsimiles of their autographs, thumbnail sketches of their lives in the big leagues, and all the latest batting averages! Come to think of it, there's even a stick of gum stuck in there somewhere. □ □

Series Books

Marvelous escapades and derring-do
with Frank and Earnest heroes

ERIES books are a most nostalgic collectible. Their pages reflect the events of their era, with story lines often drawn from banner headlines of the day. Peary, Scott and Amundsen explored the polar caps, and close on their heels came *Tom Swift (in the Caves of Ice), Dick Kent (with the Eskimos),* and *Don Sturdy (across the North Pole).* Henry Ford introduced his automobile to the world, and the Motor Boys and Motor Maids rushed out on to America's roadways to try it out. Soon after the Wright Brothers flew at Kitty Hawk, the skies were filled with the Flying Machine Boys, the Airship Boys, Dave Dashaway, Our Young

Aeroplane Scouts, and the Air Service Boys. The invention of radio gave rise to the Radio Boys, the Radio Girls, the Wireless Boys, and the Radiophone Boys. And if you were to believe what you read in *The Army Boys in the French Trenches* and *The Navy Boys Behind Big Guns,* clearly the Allies won World War I largely thanks to the efforts of a handful of series-book characters.

The first two series books on the American scene were far from stirring chronicles. In fact, the Rollo books by Jacob Abbott and the Peter Parley books by Samuel Goodrich are, by today's standards, almost incredibly tame. The author of the Rollo series, the more widely read of the two, had been a farmer, minister, teacher, historian, and amateur scientist at different times of his life, but his biggest success was as an author. Not only did his first children's story become a continuing saga (the Rollo books eventually numbered twenty-eight volumes), but so did the other stories to come from his pen. Abbott's Rainbow and Lucky series went into five volumes, the Lucy Books included six books, as did the Jonas Books. His popular *Franconia Stories* ran through ten volumes. Published originally by Boston and New York publishers over the period from 1835 to 1859, each one of these series featured characters and familiar settings that remained constant from book to book, teaching the young reader how to talk, read, write, and be entertained. "Come here, I have got some pictures to show you," Mama tells little Rollo in *The Little Scholar Learning To Talk; A Picture Book For Rollo* (1835). "Come and sit up on my lap and I will show them all to you." First editions of these gems are now commanding from $15 to $35 per volume.

The next author to succeed with the series format was William Taylor Adams, (better known as "Oliver Optic"), who published his first book, *The Boat Club,* in 1855. So popular was this initial volume, eventually running into sixty editions, that Adams came up with five more in a series. Other series followed — the Great Western series, the Onward and Upward series, and the Young Americans Abroad series, to name a few. Financial success made it possible for Adams to publish two landmark children's publications, *The Student and the Schoolmate* and *Oliver Optic's Magazine.* Their pages were filled with heart-tugging tales of youngsters who surmounted incredible odds to prove that where there's pluck, there's luck.

Writing for the first of these was Horatio Alger, Jr., son of a Massachusetts preacher. Alger's pluck-luck, rags-to-riches-through-hard-work characters epitomized the American ideal of success, and his books sold wildly in the decade following the Civil War. His stories were reprinted by more companies than any other printed material, excluding only the Bible and Webster's Dictionary. Practically every publisher of the late nineteenth century listed an Alger work, and for this reason, only the original editions published by A.K. Loring or Porter & Coates have collecting value. Most Alger first editions are now worth somewhere between $10 and $40. Reprints by such firms as Donohue, Hearst and A.L. Burt, seldom draw more than a dollar or two.

Tattered Tom and Mark the Matchboy live on at the annual

convention of the Horatio Alger Society. Members gather yearly to exchange Alger books and discuss the many methods used by Alger's heroes to climb from rags to riches. Organized in 1961, the society publishes a newsletter, *The Newsboy.* Headquarters are at 4907 Allison Drive, Lansing, MI 48910.

A prolific author of early series books for girls was Rebecca Sophia Clarke. Her first work appeared in the *Little Pilgrim* Magazine, under the pen-name "Sophie May." These weekly stories about "Little Prudy" eventually became a six-volume series, which appeared between 1863 and 1865. She went on to produce a long line of series books read by two generations, including the Dotty Dimple books, Little Prudy's Flyaway series, the Flaxie Frizzle series, and a final effort, completed shortly before her death, Little Prudy's Children series.

In 1881, Lee and Shepard published the first of what was to be another series slanted toward girl readers. *Five Little Peppers and How They Grew,* written by Harriett Mulford Stone Lothrop of New Haven, Connecticut, under the pen-name "Margaret Sidney," sold over two million copies. The books told the story of five lively children (David, Polly, Ben, Phronsie, and Joel) brought up by their widowed mother. Subsequent books in the series — *Five Little Peppers Midway* and *Five Little Peppers Grown Up* — continued the history of the Pepper family.

The year 1899 was a turning point for popular juvenile fiction. It was not one of those events heralded by trumpets and the like, but its effects were tremendous. The year 1899 saw the Rover Boys burst onto the scene. And they would move mountains. Tom, Dick and Sam Rover were introduced to the world in *The Rover Boys at School,* the first book of the famous series issued by the Mershon Company of New York. For their creator, author Edward Stratemeyer, it marked the birth of an enterprise destined to

"Laura Lee Hope" was Mrs. Howard Garis. In addition to the Bobbsey Twins, she also wrote the Motor Girls and the Bunny Brown series.

reap millions and place him at the head of a publishing empire unparalleled in the history of juvenile fiction. The Stratemeyer Syndicate, formed as a result of the success of the Rover brothers, would in time produce such characters as Tom Swift, the Bobbsey Twins, the Motor Boys, Bomba the Jungle Boy, Nancy Drew and the Hardy Boys. The Stratemeyer fiction factory cranked out a phenomenal number of popular series — stories guaranteed to hold their young readers on the edge of their seats in anticipation of the next installment in the series.

Edward Stratemeyer began writing in the style of Horatio Alger, but developed his own style in the late 1890's. During this period, the United States was in the middle of the Spanish-American War. Glowing press accounts of naval and land victories inspired Stratemeyer to produce four patriotic series, the Old Glory series, Pan-American series, Soldiers of Fortunes series and Colonial series, which were all prime movers for the Lee & Shepard company of Boston.

Moonlighting for the Mershon company while still writing for Lee & Shepard, Stratemeyer began to employ pen names to increase the circulation of his work. Among the pen names developed by Stratemeyer for his Mershon books were "Captain Ralph Bonehill," "Roy Rockwood" and "Arthur M. Winfield." Mr. Winfield, by the way, became the author of the Rover Boys books. It would be years before Edward Stratemeyer's name ever became associated with the Rover books.

Series books were to at least three generations of children a source of entertainment and excitement just as habit-forming as radio and television were later to become.

As a result of the sales of the Rover Boys books, Stratemeyer formed a syndicate headquartered in New Jersey. Shortly after this (about 1908), Stratemeyer heard about Howard Garis, a newspaper reporter who was making waves with rabbit stories for children. Stratemeyer persuaded Garis to join the syndicate and immediately set him to work on a story about young automobilists. The Motor Boys series, published under the pseudonym "Clarence Young," brought Garis a fee of $100 per book. For a girls' companion series, Stratemeyer contracted Garis' wife, Lilian, as "Margaret Penrose," who wrote the Motor Girls series.

Stratemeyer favored pen names on purely practical grounds. If one writer should die or defect from the syndicate in the middle of a series, a new writer could promptly be hired to continue the series without interruption. For all the syndicate's series, Stratemeyer himself provided his authors with brief guidelines to follow regarding the characters, settings and plots. The range was amazing. There were, of course, the famous Bobbsey Twins (Lilian Garis wrote the first volumes), the Racer Boys, Jack Ranger, College Sports, Great Marvel, Motion Picture Boys, Don Sturdy, all less well-known today, and Bomba the Jungle Boy. (The Great Marvel series was a Jules Verne-ish collection of stories about two scientific-minded boys and their professor father, who built rockets that could penetrate both earth and space.) Howard Garis is believed to have written many books in all of these series.

The best-known series Howard Garis helped produce for the

syndicate involved an inventive boy with a knack for creating fantastic gadgets. The boy's name was Tom Swift. Stratemeyer had provided Garis with the initial synopsis of the series in 1910 (the character's name was actually first used in a story Stratemeyer had written in 1897). The Tom Swift series was a smash hit right from the start, rivaling Stratemeyer's own Rover Boys in sales. Among Tom's many inventions were the electric rifle, photo telephone, wizard camera and electric locomotive. Collectors say that the Tom Swift series is the most popular of the collected series today. There is constantly a demand for Swift books, with volumes selling for between $5 and $15 each today.

Howard Garis did write a few series for the Stratemeyer Syndicate under his own name, including the twenty-volume Buddy books. But for the most part, the bulk of writing to come from him will forever be obscured by a sea of pen names. It is ironic that at the time of his death in 1962, Howard Garis was noted primarily for the rabbit stories he wrote under his own name as a young reporter in Newark. The rabbit's name, by the way, was Uncle Wiggily.

Second to the syndicate's books in popularity today are the series of Edward Edson Lee. Lee, who began as a magazine writer, possessed a keen sense of humor, which he conveyed through the characters of his books put out by Grosset & Dunlap. The Jerry Todd series (begun in 1924 with *Jerry Todd and the Whispering Mummy)* and the Poppy Ott series (launched in 1926 with *Poppy Ott and the Stuttering Parrot*) related the hometown adventures of a group of kids who encountered such creatures as waltzing hens, galloping snails and whispering mummies. The characters lived in the imaginary town of Tutter, Illinois. Other popular series by this author included the Tuffy Bean, Trigger Berg, and Andy Blake series. During the early 1930's, with the blessings of his publisher, Lee (who wrote as "Leo Edwards") formed a fan club for the readers of his stories. "The Secret and Mysterious Order of the Freckled Goldfish," as the club was called, reached a peak in 1934, when over a thousand boys and girls filled its ranks. A newspaper for these fans grown up, *The Tutter Bugle,* was published for a number of years by Robert L. Johnson, who is now preparing a bound volume of the articles, stories and photos from past *Bugles*. For information about the book or copies of the *Bugle,* write Mr. Johnson at P.O. Box 47, 25 Main Street, Bisbee, AZ 85603.

Today series-book collecting has become a growing hobby. "The hobby is divided into two categories," series-book collector Ed LeBlanc, Sr., of Fall River, Massachusetts, explained. "The first involves collecting the earliest books, those published in the nineteenth century, by Horatio Alger, Jr., 'Oliver Optic,' and their contemporaries." First editions are always more valuable than reprints. Mr. LeBlanc added, "Many libraries and universities, recognizing the important role these books played in the development of children's literature, are forming their own collections. The University of Minnesota has a huge one already."

The second branch of series-book collecting belongs to those who collect out of nostalgia, seeking the books they grew up reading. "The big era for these collectors was the period between the wars," Mr. LeBlanc said, "from the teens up to the 1940's." During this period, publishers like Grosset & Dunlap, Cupples & Leon, and A.L. Burt were issuing hundreds of series to a book-hungry young readership. "Ten years ago you could get these books for a dime or quarter at secondhand stores," Mr. LeBlanc said. "Now they sell from $2 to $3 in the bins (unsorted) and from $5 to $15 through dealers."

Ed LeBlanc currently has about five thousand books in his collection. "I have a large house and have my books shelved in three rooms upstairs," he said. He is also the editor of *The Dime Novel Roundup* (87 School Street, Fall River, MA 02720), a bimonthly publication which covers early juvenile fiction. "Our publication was begun in 1931 by Ralph F. Cummings as a magazine for dime novel collectors," he said. Mr. LeBlanc acquired it in 1956, found a new interest in series books developing and began to feature stories on hardbound children's series alongside articles about dime novels. "Today we have about four hundred subscribers, who come from around the country, as well as Canada, England, Australia and France," Mr. LeBlanc said. Members pay $5 and receive six issues a year and a bibliography. "One of our latest issues featured an article on the various formats of the Tom Swift books," he said. "Our readers do a great deal of buying and swapping among one another, sending out long want lists." One collector may want a copy of *Tom Swift in the Caves of Ice,* and be willing to part with his duplicate copy of *The Rover Boys in the Mountains* in exchange.

George Gloss of the Brattle Book Shop in Boston says that, of the ten thousand "second-hand" children's books he has in stock, his biggest sellers are the early editions of the Hardy Boys and Nancy Drew series, both begun by the Stratemeyer Syndicate a half-century ago and still in print. "Collectors come in here at a rate of 50 a week looking for certain titles and volume numbers," he said. Across the country, Bob Johnson of Prospector's Coin and Book Center in Bisbee, Arizona, sees the same thing. "Adults are actively collecting. Age, condition, and original dust jackets are what they're after." Until the late 1950's, paper dust jackets were issued on all the books, and as these were easily torn or discarded, they're now hard to find. Leo Edwards titles with dust jackets in good condition will bring up to $15-$20, particularly if autographed. Probably the most expensive collectable series book, according to Johnson, is the *Andy Blake in Advertising* published by Appleton, as a copy in mint or near mint condition could command as much as $85.

What happened to all the old series? The advent of new forms of entertainment was largely responsible for their decline, although a few still survive. "The rise of radio, Saturday afternoon movies and comic books did a lot to cut into the books' popularity in the 1940's," collector Ed LeBlanc said. "Television dealt the final blow in the 1950's." One wonders if Tom Swift knew what he was doing when he invented it back in 1914! □

Children's Sleds

The "Rosebud" Syndrome

WITH decks exquisitely hand-painted in colorful designs and floral patterns, nineteenth century sleds have a beauty all their own, much valued today by Americana collectors. In the words of one dealer, who had just sold a deluxe 1890's Rival Clipper with white ash woodwork and upholstered deck for an even $200, "those cold-weather sleds are hot items!"

A magic moment for any child is when he first becomes the proud possessor of a shiny new sled on Christmas morning. And adults seem to retain that idyllic childish dream of coasting down hills of glistening white on a frosty winter's morning on sleds whose very names breathe courage and challenge — Sky Rocket, Snow King, Champion Clipper, White Star, Snow Bird . . .

Early American sleds are found in the strangest places nowadays — in living rooms as coffee tables, on den walls as original works of folk art, in yards as lawn ornaments. "We think they're pretty," one homeowner observed about the half-dozen antique sleds adorning the roof of his house. These sleds are being collected and restored with a zeal once reserved for Chippendale furniture. The field is certainly fertile for the collector. Literally thousands of varieties were produced, from the short, squatty "bellyflopper" sleds made by the Chicago Roller Skate Company, to the long, lean, eight-man sleds made by the Kalamazoo Sled Company. Some thousand different models were on the market in the year 1900 alone.

For years, most of the children's sleds sold in this country were made in Binghamton, New York. Formed in 1860, the Binghamton sled company went through several name changes before emerging as the Wilkinson Manufacturing Company in 1890. During its hey-day, Wilkinson produced many successful lines of sleds, the leader of which was The Storm King. In the 1924 catalogue Wilkinson listed The Storm King as available in seven different sizes, from the sporty Number 60 model (measuring 28 inches long) to the extended Number 67 model (50 inches long). The old Wilkinson plant in Binghamton covered several city blocks and encompassed a sprawling collection of buildings equipped with woodworking machinery run by water power. The company continued to produce children's sleds until it went out of

Black Beauty sled.

The Snow Fairy for girls . . .

and the Hardwood Clipper for boys.

business in the 1930's. Sleds made by Wilkinson in the 1890's can often be found priced between $35 and $50.

Proclaiming itself to be "the largest producer of sleds in the world" at the turn-of-the-century, the Kalamazoo Sled Company had the sales to prove it. Noted for the sleek styling of its sleds, the company began production in 1894. Its Champion model rapidly became the fastest selling sled in the Midwest. Two other contemporary companies putting out sleds to lay under the Christmas tree were the Buffalo Sled Company (whose production peaked in 1919) and The American Toy and Novelty Works of York, Pennsylvania, makers of the Royal Racer, termed "the spirit of the hills."

Many Philadelphia-made sleds were to be found on the nation's slopes thanks to S. L. Allen & Company. Their best-known model, Flexible Flyer, featured what was perhaps the single biggest advancement in the history of sled production, a steering mechanism. Before the Flexible Flyer was developed in 1889 (created by S. L. Allen himself, for his daughter), the only way you could steer a sled was by leaning into the desired direction and dragging the tips of your feet. But now, thanks to a simple suspension device mounted on the front of the Flexible Flyer, steering was as simple as tugging on one side or the other of the wooden steering bar and cutting a fine turn. Kids who showed up on the slopes with these new sleds were the envy of the neighborhood, and it's little wonder that other companies quickly followed suit with steering sleds of their own. Made in nine sizes, the Flexible Flyer appealed to buyers nationally with glowing advertisements. A 1917 Flexible Flyer ad promised speed ("You'll be the winner in every race"), parental approval ("Tell Mother and Father that you don't have to drag your feet steering, get them wet and wear out shoes") and even medicinal benefits ("It prevents colds and saves on doctors' bills").

Sleds made in the Northeast are today considered "the cream of the crop" among the collectable antique sleds. Antique shops around the New England area have become meccas for collectors all across the country who dream of uncovering a treasure like the white ash Snow Fairy, once called "the most beautiful sled on earth." Because of their superb, ingenious design and beautifully painted decks, many early New England sleds command prices of up to $200 — for example, the sleds manufactured by the Paris Manufacturing Company of South Paris, Maine; by Colby Brothers & Company of Waterbury, Vermont; and by the Vermont Novelty Works of Springfield, Vermont. During the nineteenth century each of these firms had its own showroom on Broadway in New York City.

Sleds by the Colby Brothers are among the oldest being collected today. "Manufacturers of Sleds, Sleighs and Clippers in Elegant Styles," an 1870 ad announced. Many Colby sleds date back to before the Civil War. During its peak years (1860's and 1870's), Colby employed over a hundred people working in fifteen shop buildings around the clock. Until it went out of busi-

When You and I Were Young/*Children's Sleds*

ness in 1876, the company specialized in sleds noted for their low, uniform styling. These sleds sell today for $175-$200 if in top condition.

Sleds made by Colby's chief in-state rival, the Vermont Novelty Works, are also prized collectibles. More elaborate than most, the Springfield sleds (produced between 1858 and 1895) were often graced with gooseneck runners. They bring prices ranging from $95 to $150. Considering that the factory was totally destroyed twice by flood (1864 and 1869) and once by fire (1878), it is a wonder that any Vermont Novelty Works sleds exist at all today. During the 1869 flood, company sleds by the hundreds went floating down the Connecticut River. Other Vermont sled companies included Clark & Havens of Poultney and S. A. Smith & Company of Guilford.

Sleds made by these Vermont firms are today considered museum pieces.

One of the most ingenious sleds ever created was the roller-runner Whizzard, offered by the Pollack Roller Runner Sled Company of Boston for the then high price of $10 apiece. Each Whizzard featured tiny metal wheels built into the runners for added speed. Called an "all-season sled," the Whizzard could be used in summer as well as in winter. "You never in your life saw a sled like this one!" a 1927 ad said. "It rolls as well as slides! Little wheels in Whizzard runners make it go like sixty — snow or no snow — it's all the same to a Whizzard." But it wasn't all the same to young sledders. The idea of sledding in the summer never caught on, and despite massive advertising, few roller-runner sleds were sold. This is reflected in the relative scarcity of Whizzard sleds today. Models from as late as the 1920's have sold for $25-$35 at recent auctions.

Other companies also marketed roller-runner sleds, with mixed results. S. L. Allen & Company of Philadelphia produced a wheeled sled, called the "Flexy Racer." These were accorded a certain amount of popularity and today sell for $15-$20.

Of all the early sled companies, one firm has stood the test of time. Known for many years as the Paris Manufacturing Company of South Paris, Maine, the firm has remained under the direction of the same family since 1861. Owned since 1970 by the Gladding Corporation, a recreation empire based in South Otselic, New York, the South Paris sleds works has survived to see its earliest products now considered valuable antiques. Henry R. Morton, who is vice-president and general manager in charge of Gladding's Wood & Youth Products Division, is the great-grandson of the original company's founder, Henry F. Morton. "Those old sleds were really works of art," Mr. Morton told me during my visit. "In the old days we used to hire artistic local people who would sit around huge lazy Susans painting flowers and birds on sleds all day long." There were many variations, he explained, as every painter added a little something different as each sled came around. Mr. Morton is rather amused by the current status of the old Paris Manufacturing sleds as collector's items. "It's funny — we sold

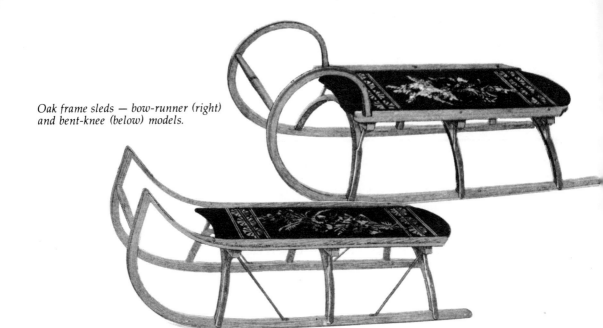

Oak frame sleds — bow-runner (right)
and bent-knee (below) models.

some of our old clippers for six dollars a dozen then. Today they turn up at auctions for a couple of hundred dollars apiece. Too bad we didn't hold on to some of them!"

Antique shops within a wide radius of South Paris are besieged with requests for early Paris clippers and frame sleds. "They're extremely popular and always in demand," said Pixie Cushman of the Turner Center Antique Shop in Turner, Maine. "The beautiful lines and hand-painted decorations of the Paris sleds make them awfully good sellers. They sell just as fast as we can get our hands on them, which isn't easy. We haven't had one in eight months." A similar phenomenon is reported by Ann Mc-Crillis of the Yankee Gem Corporation of Roxbury, Maine, dealers in Americana. Paris sleds constantly outsell other makes, reports Berdan's Antiques of Hallowell, Maine. "The first thing people do when they see a sled is check along the underside for the stamped words, 'Paris Manufacturing Company'."

The 1890's saw the Paris Manufacturing Company rise to national prominence. The South Paris plant was greatly expanded in 1897, and a branch was opened in New York City. Soon showrooms were appearing in such diverse places as Baltimore, Chicago, and San Francisco (where half the fun must have been trying to explain what a sled was used for). The South Paris building was kept in spit-and-polish condition as there was no telling who might drop by. Among frequent visitors to the plant were some of the world's noted Arctic and Antarctic explorers. Both MacMillan and Admiral Peary used South Paris sleds on many of their Arctic treks — a fact which the company did not hesitate to emphasize in its advertising. MacMillan wired from the northern tip of Greenland in 1914, "Your sled has covered about 2000 miles up to date and is without a crack."

During the early years of the twentieth century, Paris Manufacturing was producing two styles of fast-selling sleds — clipper sleds for boys and frame model sleds for girls. The sturdy clippers

When You and I Were Young/*Children's Sleds*

were built close to the ground for speed, and usually decorated with painted eagles, leaping deer and galloping horses. The higher-built, slower frame sleds featured colorful rosebuds, birds and cherubs emblazoned on the deck. For years the most famous clipper, the Black Beauty, sold for about $2 each. The top-selling frame sled was the Snow Fairy, which measured 32 inches long, had two tinkling bells attached to its upswirled runners, and cost $4. Other popular sleds found in the company's turn-of-the-century catalogues included: the Champion Clipper, distinguished by the bald eagle painted on its oaken deck and dubbed the ne plus ultra of boys' sleds; the Paris Racer, "built for speed;" the White Star, "copied by every sled-maker in the country;" and the Rival Clipper, with a deck luxuriously upholstered in leather.

None of these early sleds had any steering device. Following the lead of S. L. Allen & Company, Paris Manufacturing introduced steerable sleds in the 1920's — first the Speedaway, then the Speedster. With the advent of the Flexible Flyer, steering sleds had become the wave of the future; soon the old clippers and frame sleds disappeared into the footnotes of sled-making history.

Today the old South Paris sled works has been expanded by 75,000 square feet, acquired a new warehouse, and has a modernized assembly line. The company today is the world's foremost producer of children's sleds (turning out several thousand yearly) and continues to use only Maine wood, primarily maple and oak. The entire process from raw log to finished product takes about five weeks.

In collecting old sleds, there are a few points to remember. Never attempt to repaint an old sled yourself. This can greatly reduce its worth. Most collectors feel that it is better to have a half a bald eagle on a sled's deck than no eagle at all — or worse, a doctored-up version of the original. In case the paint is entirely gone (sleds kept outdoors for long periods of time are often found in this condition), it is permissible to refinish the woodwork and apply a clear lacquer to protect the wood. If you purchase a sled that has been repainted, check the deck carefully. Repainting can often conceal new boards used to replace original broken decks. Sleds that have seen such repair are of course not worth as much as those retaining the original woodwork. *Original* sleds are the ones that bring $200 or more. (An upholstered nineteenth century wooden push sled with brass runners recently sold for $275!)

Winter and children sledding go together, and for over a century American sled companies have provided the children of this country with an incredible selection of sleds with which to challenge that backyard snowbank. From clipper sleds to frame sleds, painted sleds to upholstered sleds, sleds for rolling and sleds for sliding — they're all being collected today. But to many sled collectors, their fascination is not so much that antique sleds are valuable, but rather that the images evoked by such sleds are *in*valuable — faintly recapturing halcyon childhood days. Remember that the mysterious "Rosebud," which represented to millionaire Citizen Kane (in the movie of that name) his lost happiness, was — a sled. □ □

Appendix

Some publications of interest to collectors (information on specific-category publications is given in the pertinent chapters of this book).

COLLECTORS' JOURNALS — TABLOIDS

American Collector

13920 Mt. McClellan Boulevard, Reno, Nevada, 89506. Monthly; $1/issue or $10/year. Primarily Americana; articles both inform and report; extensive classified section; calendar of events.

American Collector's Journal

PO Box 1431, Porterville, California 93257. Monthly; $7.25/year. Mostly classified ads for Americana and collectibles of all kinds.

Antique and Collector's Mart

15100 West Kellogg, Wichita, Kansas 67235. Monthly; $1/issue or $10/year. Articles both inform and report; three-page classified section; antique shop directory; calendar of events; mid-West emphasis.

Antique Gazette

929 Davidson Drive, Nashville, Tennessee 37205. Bi-monthly; $1/issue or $6/year. Extensive classified section; calendar of shows; feature articles and news; "Antique Locator;" southern emphasis.

The Antique Trader Weekly

Box 1050, Dubuque, Iowa 52001. Weekly; 75¢/issue or $17/year. Very extensive classified section; auction announcements; articles (primarily informative); "Antiqualendar."

A Page Out of History

114500 Bissonnet #301, Houston, Texas 77099. Monthly; $1/issue or $6/year. "A Collector's Shopper, Mail Auction, and Source for Books Dealing with Collectables;" includes classified section.

Collectors Journal

421 First Avenue, Box 601, Vinton, Iowa 52349. Weekly (50 issues), 25¢/issue or $12.50/year. Classified; calendar of events; news of shows and sales. Iowa and mid-West emphasis.

Collectors News

Box 156, Grundy Center, Iowa 50638. Monthly, $1/issue or $9/year. Very extensive classified section covers more than sixty different types of collectible; also includes a "dealer directory," articles about collectibles, reports of shows and sales, and other news of interest to collectors; calendar of events (national).

The Collector

Drawer C, Kermit, Texas 79745. Monthly, 75¢/issue or $8/year. Informative articles, shows and sales calendar (national), classified section, news of interest to collectors.

Maine Antiques Digest

Box 358, Waldoboro, Maine 04572. Monthly, $2/issue or $19/year. Specializes in Americana and quality antiques. Articles and news of shows, sales, museum exhibits. Many photos in both editorial and ads; limited classified section; calendar of events; many dealer advertisements and auction announcements.

Ohio Antique Review

PO Box 538, Worthington, Ohio 43085. Monthly (except January), $1/issue; $12/year second-class delivery or $30/year first-class delivery. Regional emphasis — in format similar to *Maine Antiques Digest*.

Tri-State Trader

PO Box 90, 27 North Jefferson, Knightstown, Indiana 46148. Weekly (except Christmas week), 50¢/issue or $10.50/year. "Hobby, antique, auction, and collectors' newspaper for Ohio, Kentucky, Indiana, Michigan, Illinois, western Pennsylvania, West Virginia, Tennessee, Wisconsin, Missouri, New York." Three to four pages of classified, classified genealogy section, news, articles, announcements, calendar.

The Wooden Nutmeg

Glastonbury Citizen, Inc., PO Box 504,

Glastonbury, Connecticut 06833. Bi-weekly, 50¢/issue or $7/year. Limited classified, calendar, news of shows and sales in the Northeast. Antiques and Americana primarily. Articles inform and report.

NEWSLETTER

Kovels on Antiques and Collectables

Antiques, Inc., PO Box 22200, Beachwood, Ohio 44122. Monthly, $20/year. Reports of prices paid for antiques and collectibles, short how-to articles and information helpful to collectors.

MAGAZINES

Americana

Americana Magazine, Ltd., 475 Park Avenue South, New York, New York 10016. Subscriptions: 381 West Center Street, Marion, Ohio 43302. Bi-monthly, $2.50/issue or $11.90/year. Articles of antique and Americana interest combined with historical and how-to pieces on old-time crafts and skills; short classified section.

The Antiques Journal

PO Box 1046, Dubuque, Iowa 52001. Monthly, $1.25/issue or $9/year. Magazine adjunct of *The Antique Trader Weekly*. Articles and classified concerned with collectibles of all kinds; current prices and events, dealer directory.

Early American Life

Early American Society, Inc., Gettysburg, Pennsylvania 17325. Subscriptions: PO Box 5324, Boulder, Colorado 80321. Bi-monthly, $1.50/issue or $9/year. Articles on collecting, restoration, old-time life, history, and how-to, calendar of events, classified, readers' exchange.

Spinning Wheel

Everybody's Press, Inc., *Spinning Wheel* Division, Hanover, Pennsylvania 17331. Monthly (10 times a year), $1.50/issue or $12/year. Articles and news concerning antiques and collectibles, craftsmen; some how-to's; listing of shows and shops; classified.

BOOKS ON SPECIFIC SUBJECTS

There have been a large number of books published through the years on the subjects covered in the various chapters of this book. Some of these have been well-written, competent sources, others have not been. The books listed here are those I found most helpful in preparing this volume. They were suggested to me by collectors as required reading in their different fields, and I in turn recommend them

to readers who would like to learn more about the collectibles they become acquainted with in this book. They are listed here by category.

Circus ...

Pictorial History of the American Circus, by John and Alice Durant, A. S. Barnes and Company, Cranbury, NJ, 1957.

Sheet music ...

Old Sheet Music, by Marion Klamkin, Hawthorn Books, Inc., New York, 1975.

Sunday Funnies ...

The World Encyclopedia of Comics, edited by Maurice Horn, Avon, New York, 1976.

The Comics: An Illustrated History of Comic Strip Art, by Jerry Robinson, G. P. Putnam's Sons, New York, 1974.

Photographica ...

Collecting Photographica, by George Gilbert, Hawthorn Books, Inc., New York, 1976.

Telephones ...

The Telephone Book, by H. M. Boettinger, Riverwood Publishing Company, Croton-on-Hudson, NY, 1977.

Phonographs ...

The Fabulous Phonograph, by Roland Gelatt, MacMillan, Inc., New York, 1972.

Music Boxes ...

Encyclopedia of Automatic Musical Instruments, by Q. David Bowers, Vestal Press, New York, 1972.

Christmas ...

The Santa Claus Book, by E. Willis Jones, Walker and Company, New York, 1976.

Valentines ...

A History of Valentines, by Ruth Webb Lee, The Studio Publishing Company, Inc., in association with Thomas Y. Crowell Company, New York and London, 1952.

The Romance of Greeting Cards, by Ernest Dudley Chase, Rust Craft Publishers, 1956.

Halloween ...

Halloween: Its Origin, Spirit, Celebration, and Significance, compiled and edited by Robert Haven Schaeuffer, Dodd, Mead and Company, New York, 1933.

Railroadiana ...

Railroadiana: The Collector's Guide to Railroad Memorabilia, by Charles Klamkin, Funk and Wagnalls, New York, 1976.

Baseball Cards ...

The Great American Baseball Card Flipping, Trading, and Bubble Gum Book, by Brendan C. Boyd, Little, Brown and Company, Boston, 1973.

Credits and Courtesies

Manufacturing Company, Framingham, Massachusetts.

p. 83, right; pp. 84-85 — Courtesy of Charles Jordan. Photos by Carole Allen.

p. 87; pp. 89-92; p. 94 — Courtesy of Yankee, Incorporated. Photos by Carole Allen.

p. 96 — Courtesy of Yankee, Incorporated.

pp. 98-99 — Courtesy of the Chandler Cobb Collection. Photos by Carole Allen.

p. 99, right; p. 100 — Courtesy of Charles Jordan.

p. 101 — Courtesy of Hilliard B. Holbrook, II. Photos by Carole Allen.

p. 103, below — Photos by Carole Allen.

p. 104; p. 105, right; p. 107; p. 110 — Courtesy of W. C. Williams. Photos by Frank Cordelle.

p. 105, left — Courtesy of Alan D. Haas.

p. 106, right top and bottom; p. 108 — Courtesy of the Sanborn Collection. Photos by Charles Jordan.

p. 106, right center — Courtesy of the Museum of Transportation, Boston, Massachusetts.

p. 109 — Courtesy of the Blackington Collection. Photo by Alton Hall Blackington.

p. 112 — Courtesy of Yankee, Incorporated.

p. 113; p. 115, left — Courtesy of Charles Jordan.

p. 115, right above and below — Courtesy of Judith Lund. Photos by Judith Lund.

pp. 116-118 — Photos by Carole Allen.

p. 119 — Courtesy of Charles Jordan.

p. 120 — Courtesy of Lilian Baker Carlisle. Photo by Lilian Baker Carlisle.

p. 121 — Courtesy of the Francestown Historical Society, Francestown, New Hampshire. Photo by Carole Allen.

p. 122 — Courtesy of Yankee, Incorporated.

p. 123, top — Photo by Carole Allen.

p. 123, below — Photo by Martha Burleigh.

p. 124, right — Courtesy of Nathanael Greene. Photo by Carole Allen.

p. 125, left — Courtesy of the Adirondack Museum, Blue Mountain Lake, New York. Kindness of Lilian Baker Carlisle.

pp. 128-134 — Courtesy of the Carl Terison, Jr. Collection. Photos by Stephen T. Whitney.

p. 135 — Courtesy of the Blackington Collection. Photo by Alton Hall Blackington.

pp. 137-140 — Baseball cards courtesy of the Walter Snitko Collection. Photos by Carole Allen.

p. 143; pp. 145-147 — Courtesy of Charles Jordan. Photos by Precision Industrial Photography.

pp. 150-151; p. 154 — From a 1915 General Catalog of the Paris Manufacturing Company of South Paris, Maine, courtesy of Peter D. Quinn. Photos by Carole Allen.